The ABCs of Ohio Weather
(A TV Weather-Watcher's Guide)

by Mike Davis
Chief Meteorologist, WBNS 10TV
Columbus, Ohio

Englefield and Arnold Publishing
Columbus, OH U.S.A.

Cindi Englefield Arnold, President/Publisher
Eloise Boehm-Sasala, Vice President/Managing Editor
Mercedes Baltzell, Production Editor
Jennifer King, Graphic Artist/Cover Designer
Bethany Hansgen, Project Editor
Scott Stuckey, Project Editor

Library of Congress Cataloging-in-Publication Data

Davis, Michael George, 1959-
  The ABCs of Ohio weather : a tv weather-watcher's guide / by Mike Davis.
    p. cm.
Includes bibliographical references and index.
  ISBN 1-884183-59-X (pbk.)
  1. Ohio--Climate 2. Weather. I. Title.
  QC984.O3 D38 2001
  651.69771--dc21

                              2001001523

Published by:
Englefield and Arnold Publishing • P.O. Box 341348 • Columbus, OH 43234-1348
Phone: 614-764-1211

Copyright © 2001

Printed in the United States of America
05 04 03 02 01   10 9 8 7 6 5 4 3 2 1

ISBN: 1-884183-59-X

Limit of Liability/Disclaimer of Warranty: The author and publisher have used their best
efforts in preparing this book. Englefield and Arnold, Inc., and the author make no
representation or warranties with respect to the contents of this book and specifically
disclaim any implied warranties and shall in no event be liable for any loss of any kind
including but not limited to special, incidental, consequential, or other damages.

About the Author

Mike Davis is the multiple Emmy-Winning Chief Meteorologist at WBNS 10TV in Columbus, Ohio, where he's been since 1987.

A husband and father of three, Mike is passionate about education and loves visiting schools and talking to groups about weather.

He also enjoys writing, contributing a regular column in the *Columbus Dispatch*. He has also written for the "This Week" newspapers and enjoys reading and writing science fiction.

Mike worked at TV stations in Minnesota, Idaho, and Las Vegas, before coming to Ohio. He graduated from the University of Minnesota with a degree in Journalism and studied meteorology at The Ohio State University.

Mike has won numerous Associated Press awards for his weather broadcasts including "Best Regularly Scheduled Weather" and "Best Weather Operation."

This book has been a pet project of his for several years.

Acknowledgements and Dedications

I want to extend heartfelt thanks to some of the many folks who made this long-time pet project a reality.

To my lovely wife Tama, for her unceasing inspiration and support,

To my three children Tyler, Kenzie and Logan for bringing me to every class they've ever been in... and teaching me about the joy of learning,

To Cindi Arnold, my friend and publisher, for realizing potential and plunging in headfirst,

To Joe Holbrook, friend and mentor, for leading by example and being a tough act to follow,

To WBNS 10TV for bringing me to Central Ohio in 1987 (the year the Twins won their first World Series) and for supporting and nurturing my career and passion for the weather,

To my folks, Jim and Shirley, who to this day still don't believe I do what I do,

To my first set of classmates at the University of Minnesota. Although I was graduating from journalism school, they voted me most likely to be a TV weatherman. What did they know that I didn't?

To The Ohio State University for teaching me what I needed to know to do what I do.

And, to all the viewers who get their weather, day-in and day-out, from TV. Hopefully it'll all be a little easier from here on out.

May all your days be sunny!

Mike Davis

A Letter From the Author

Weather is a paradox. Research shows that it's the #1 thing people want in local TV news. It's also, in all likelihood, the least understood part of the news. Why? Again, it's the nature of the beast. The basic idea is to take a science that's incredibly complex, and break it down into the simplest of conclusions. Will it rain? Will it snow? Will the Sun shine?

Sure, it sounds simple. But, in fact, the difference between a sunny afternoon and a cloudy one, or between rain, freezing rain, and snow, can often be a VERY fine line indeed!

As a meteorologist, it's my job to make the call. It's my job to try to predict the inherently unpredictable. So be it… But picture this. You tune into the evening news one night and out of my mouth comes, "Following a period of negative vorticity advection, we can anticipate rapidly increasing vorticity and an influx of moisture at the 700 millibar level. That, combined with a rising lifted index and CAPE values, a tight pressure gradient, not to mention disturbing changes in the 500mb–1000mb thickness contours, will result in considerable vertical instability coinciding with the period of maximum diurnal insolation." What's the first thing you'd do? Well, you'd probably **change the channel!** It's either that or go get some aspirin. But don't worry. That won't happen. (But that is the scientific jargon of our business.)

What this book is about is to try and explain some of the complexities of this tremendous heat engine we call the atmosphere. I also want to delve into the many elements (pardon the pun), terminology, and principles that you see everyday if you watch the weather on TV.

Despite the web, and the proliferation of electronic media, TV is still overwhelmingly where people turn when they want to hear about the weather. My goal here is to make it fun, understandable, and informative. And I'm going to try to cover all the bases… from A to Z.

Enjoy!

Mike Davis

ADVISORY

Meteorologists always seem to be putting out some kind of advisory. But it's all in an effort to give you plenty of notice about changing weather conditions. Advisories are reserved for less severe weather events which may cover a large area and make for difficult or dangerous travel conditions.

ALBERTA CLIPPER

Here's one of those terms we Ohioans have come to know and love, especially during the late fall and early winter months. Not to be confused with *Columbus Clippers* (the minor league baseball team that calls Columbus, Ohio, home), this "clipper" is a fast-moving storm that originates over Canada's Alberta province and then dives down across the Midwest and Great Lakes regions on its fast track eastward. Since these storms usually move very quickly, they typically produce only light to moderate snowfall, while often leaving behind sharply cooler temperatures. It's also one of our favorite winter buzzwords.

ALMANAC

Almanacs, especially the venerable *Old Farmer's Almanac*, could be characterized as a forecasting alternative to the modern meteorologist. Lots of folks swear by 'em. The term itself, however, is thought to be of Arabic origin, meaning "calendar of the heavens." Almanacs have fascinated us for centuries with their anecdotes, astrology, astronomy, advertisements, and assorted events... not to mention weather forecasts. The *Old Farmer's Almanac* celebrated its 200th birthday in 1992.

When we use the term "almanac" on the air, it is to show historical information about our climate, such as record high and low temperatures, last year's high and low temperatures for the day, and normal highs and lows.

I once read about a fictitious part of the forecast called "Yearagostats." This is the part of the forecast that tells you what it was like this time last year… so that you'll feel even more miserable.

AMS

Those three letters turn up all the time when you're watching the weather. Sometimes, you see them after the meteorologist's name, and sometimes, even on the weather maps. They must stand for something. Not to be confused with the AMA, which represents doctors, AMS stands for American Meteorological Society. The AMS is a voluntary, non-profit organization that promotes the study and advancement of atmospheric sciences.

AMS SEAL

The AMS seal is the official mascot of the American Meteorological Society. **Just kidding.** The AMS Seal of Approval is awarded to broadcast meteorologists who meet certain standards set forth by the AMS. These standards include edu-

cational background, on-air performance, communication, and forecasting skills. Given the changing nature of our business, and the technological advances being made every day, these standards change with time in order to reflect current levels of expertise.

ANVIL

The top portion of towering thunderstorm clouds sometimes takes the shape of a blacksmith's monstrous anvil... you know, the kind you saw smithies using to bang out horseshoes in those old Westerns. They flatten out against the tropopause, which is at the top of the lower part of our atmosphere (the part containing the air, clouds, and weather) and is about 11 miles up.

Sometimes, the flat part of the anvil spreads out for hundreds of miles. Impressive as it is, the anvil is actually the mature or dying stage of a big thunderstorm. When isolated in the distance, these anvils can be among the most impressive sights in nature.

H. Michael Mogil

North Carolina coastal thunderstorm

ASOS

Here's one you probably haven't heard of before. ASOS is an acronym for **A**utomated **S**urface **O**bserving **S**ystem. One is located at Port Columbus International Airport and most of the other surface stations around the state. They're part of a national network of automated weather instruments that collect data 24 hours a day. When the National Weather Service reorganized a few years ago, a lot of personnel in the field simply went away, only to be replaced by ASOS. While the network provides data for places that might not otherwise report it, they do have their limitations, especially when it comes to sky conditions and snowfall.

ATMOSPHERE (THE AIR)

This is where all the weather happens. Without an atmosphere, there would be no weather. Our atmosphere is made up of about three-fourths nitrogen, one-fourth oxygen, and small amounts of water vapor, carbon dioxide, argon, and trace gases. I think it surprises people that nitrogen, at 78%, easily beats oxygen, at 21%, as the main ingredient of our air. But we, as meteorologists, are concerned with the way the atmosphere moves. It probably comes as no surprise, but our atmosphere is **very active**. The reason for all this activity is the difference in heating from place to place and the resulting differences in atmospheric pressure. (see **Barometric Pressure**)

The part of the atmosphere where we live and breathe, better known as "the air," only extends for about ten miles above the Earth's surface. And only the force of gravity keeps it from flying off into space. Just to put it in perspective, if the Earth was an apple, our atmosphere would be thinner than the skin of the apple!

AURORA BOREALIS

Every once in a while, we catch a glimpse of this northerly phenomenon, also known as the northern lights. And, when somebody does, they usually call the TV station to report "strange lights in the sky." Well, strange they are, at least for longtime Buckeyes.

The northern lights are caused by charged particles from the Sun entering the Earth's magnetic shield over the poles, where they collide with various gases in the atmosphere. The resulting display can take many forms: from arcs, to rays, to something that almost looks like shimmering curtains of light. The most common aurora colors are white, red, green, and gold. While typically confined to the polar regions, these colorful displays can occasionally be seen on clear nights here in Ohio (though it is a fairly rare occurrence).

The aurora borealis made a nice appearance in November 1991. On these rare occasions, VHF and FM radio broadcasts may be affected. There is a similar phenomenon in the Southern Hemisphere called the "aurora australis." Both occur at more than 30 miles above the surface of the Earth where these *solar storms* interact with the thin atmosphere.

AUTUMNAL EQUINOX

Welcome to fall. The date is on or about September 22nd. It's that time of year when the Sun is now directly above the equator and days and nights are close to the same length around the world. Here in Ohio, the Sun is close to 50 degrees above the southern horizon at noon. The autumnal equinox marks the official beginning of fall. However, meteorologists generally consider fall as September through November and winter as December to February, for all practical purposes.

The seasons result from the Earth's journey around the Sun and the Earth's 23 ½ degree tilt. But why do we have to bid farewell to Summer? Well, the North Pole is now tilted away from the Sun. By December 21st — the winter solstice — the Earth is tilted the full 23 ½ degrees away from the Sun. Of course, with the change of seasons upon us, can the first frost be far behind? On average, Columbus hits its first 32°F temperature around October 17th. Delaware, London, Newark, Marion, Marysville, Circleville, and Lancaster tend to see it a little bit earlier. Others later. (see **Freeze, First & Last**)

Keep in mind, though, averages are just that. They should be used only as general guidelines. Even averages are revised periodically, every ten years or so, based upon 30-year averages. Anyway, if these were hard and fast rules, who'd need the daily forecast anyway?

BACKSIDE OF THE LOW

I'm convinced that this is my ol' pal Dave Kaylor's favorite
weather term. Dave has worked next to me on the anchor desk at
Channel 10 since 1987. He maintains that his own personal
"swami" told him all about it. That's why he likes to throw it
around during my forecast. As much as I hate to admit it, he's
right! It's an especially helpful term for explaining why wet or
snowy weather comes and goes in Ohio.

Air circulates around low pressure in a counter-clockwise
direction. Say that a low pressure and a cold front sweep across
the northern part of the state. We may get rain or snow from the
passing front before it starts to clear up. That's where the backside
of the low comes in. Air moving counter-clockwise around the
low dives down across the Great Lakes, often picking up moisture
and producing clouds (which may mean even more rain or snow
for the state). Just when you thought you were out of the woods!

Since this air is moving southward out of Canada, our air also
tends to cool off as the low slides off to the east.

Motto: Beware the backside of the low!

BAROMETRIC PRESSURE

Barometric pressure, also known as atmospheric pressure, is the
force exerted by the weight of the air. Pressure is also a driving
force behind the weather. Think of it this way. Air is a fluid, just
like water. If you scoop a bucket of water out of the tub, what

happens? Are you left with a hole in the water? Of course not. More water rushes in, causing ripples or waves, before eventually evening out again. But when it comes to the air, things never really iron out. Not entirely.

In an effort to reach equilibrium, air rushes from high pressure into low pressure in an attempt to fill it up. But that only creates another low pressure area which, of course, needs filling! And this goes on, and on, and on! It's a vicious cycle! As such, pressure is the driving force behind the wind. Rapid pressure changes create strong winds.

Here's a little rule of thumb: Sometime, when you're outside, stand with your back to the wind. Low pressure will be on your left, while high pressure is to your right. Of course, this is only true in the Northern Hemisphere. If you are ever south of the equator, it's the reverse.

On the news, we report the barometric pressure in inches of mercury. (That's how far mercury in a glass tube will rise up based on the weight of the atmosphere pushing down upon it.) It rises and falls naturally during the course of a day. Typically, it has low points around 4:00 a.m. and 4:00 p.m. and high points at 10:00 a.m. and 10:00 p.m. What we, as forecasters, look for are rapid changes that signal approaching fronts and, potentially, stormy weather.

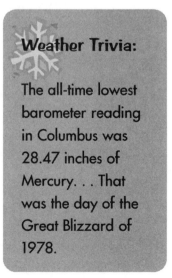

Weather Trivia:

The all-time lowest barometer reading in Columbus was 28.47 inches of Mercury. . . That was the day of the Great Blizzard of 1978.

BLACK ICE

Black ice is an all but invisible road hazard in the winter. It's a layer of seemingly invisible ice that's, for all intents and purposes, indistinguishable from the roadway until you hit it and lose control of your vehicle.

BLIZZARD

The term blizzard seems to confuse a lot of people. Most long-time residents of Ohio have not forgotten the blizzard of 1978. But there was a much more recent blizzard, the blizzard of March 13–14, 1993. Funny thing is, a number of people seemed disappointed by that one. Not the folks in southeastern Ohio, many of whom saw over two feet of snowfall combined with blowing and drifting that created five-foot drifts and paralyzed some rural areas for days. But in the Columbus area, the blizzard just wasn't snowy enough for some people. Blizzards aren't about big-time snow. They're about blowing snow, poor visibility, and bitter cold. (see **Blizzard Warning**)

BLIZZARD WARNING

A blizzard warning is issued when sustained or gusty winds of 35 miles per hour or more, combined with falling and blowing snow, are expected to reduce visibility to a quarter mile or less. These *white out* conditions are expected to last **at least** three hours.

BLIZZARD BOWL

Here's one that tells you everything you need to know about those die-hard Buckeye football fans. The date was November 25, 1950… just another game day, right? Absolutely not! It was "Michigan" Saturday, and that year, the Buckeyes were hosting their arch rivals, the Michigan Wolverines.

Also referred to as the Snow Bowl and the Ice Bowl (though I think Blizzard Bowl has the best ring to it), this pivotal game took place at the height of the great Thanksgiving week snowstorm of 1950, one of the biggest and longest-lasting snowstorms in Ohio history.

Did they cancel the game? Heck no. We're talking BUCKEYE FOOTBALL here. Despite the protests of Ohio State coach Wes Fesler, kickoff took place against gale force winds, blinding snows, and a wind chill approaching -40°F.

The players couldn't see the yard markers, and the Buckeye faithful in "B" and "C" decks at the Horseshoe couldn't even see the field!

Future Heisman Trophy winner Vic Janowicz punted the ball an amazing 21 times! He also made the longest gain of the day, a whopping 11 yards. Janowicz remarked that it was more like skating than running on the "field" that day.

To add insult to injury, the Bucks blew the Blizzard Bowl 9-3, in a game where the Maize and Blue had no completed passes and no first downs. The loss cost the Scarlet and Gray a trip to the Rose Bowl, and Fesler took flack for some of his decisions that afternoon.

And just to show the kind of impact that weather can have on life in general, Fesler quit about a month later, paving the way for a young upstart from Miami of Ohio named… Woody Hayes!

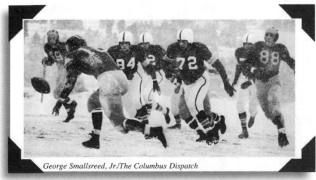

George Smallsreed, Jr./The Columbus Dispatch

The Blizzard Bowl of 1950.

BLIZZARD OF JANUARY 26–27, 1978

These are days that no one who lived in Ohio at the time will ever forget. By the time the great blizzard struck on January 26th, it had already been a record setting month in Columbus. By January 20th, the monthly snowfall at Port Columbus had set a new record: 29.4 inches. This smashed the old record, set in 1918, by four inches! The snow depth at the airport on the 20th of January was 17 inches. That was the most snow on the ground ever at one time since records began in 1878.

The day before the blizzard was a quiet one. Through 7:00 that evening, the temperature hovered at 38°F. Winds were light and out of the northeast. Then, the barometer started to plummet. After dark, it started to rain. By 10:00 p.m., the temperature was up to 39°F, the rain had gotten heavy, and the barometer continued its steep drop. Between 11:00 p.m. and midnight, the thermometer rose to 41°F. By this point, the barometric pressure had long since surpassed the all-time record low.

The day of the blizzard was one to remember. Between 1:00 a.m. and 2:00 a.m., the temperature dropped to 36°F and nearly three-quarters of an inch of rain had fallen in just two hours. At 1:22 a.m., the barometer hit 28.47, its lowest point ever in Columbus, breaking the old record by 0.4 inches! Then, between 2:00 a.m. and 3:00 a.m. the temperature hit freezing. Rain turned to snow, and the winds were up to 35 miles per hour (mph). At 3:31 a.m., the winds hit 69 mph.

Picture this. In just 2 ½ hours, the temperature had dropped 20 degrees, and the winds had gone from 5 mph to 69 mph! The winds kept up, and the blizzard raged through the morning hours. The snow depth which was a compacted three inches at 1:00 p.m., climbed to six inches by midnight Thursday night. But one of the biggest problems from the blizzard was a thick layer of ice caused by the fast-frozen, heavy rain.

This house, under construction, collapsed under the weight of snow shortly after the 1978 Blizzard.

BLUE MOON

You've heard the expression "once in a blue moon." That tells you they don't happen all that often. But what are they? For well over 50 years, most of us thought the "blue moon" was the second full moon of the month. WRONG. And this little mistake not only left some journalists feeling blue, but also a bit red in the face.

Back in the mid 1940s, a popular astronomy magazine published an article stating that the "blue moon" was the second full moon of the month. What the author meant to say was that the "blue moon" is the third full moon in a season containing four full moons.

Typically, each season only has three full moons. By the way, "blue moons" are only found in February, May, August, and November, in other words, months that come late in the various seasons.

Funny thing is, it **isn't** blue. In fact, I can't find any reason as to why it's called a "blue moon." Still, regardless of the above faux pas, most still think of the blue moon as the second full moon of the month… something that only occurs every 2.7 years! In other words, don't hold your breath waiting, or it'll be you turning blue! It does make for a catchy tune, though.

BLUE SCREEN

It used to be a great mystery to people. But then the Center of Science and Industry (COSI) in Columbus, Ohio, and others came along and gave away one of our great little secrets. But for those of you who don't already know, it only looks like the TV weather person is standing in front of a map. Actually, it's just a blank blue (sometimes green) wall. It's called a **chromakey**. And it's not really a screen at all, since nothing is projected onto it. But, to the viewer, there's the illusion that a meteorologist is standing in front of a physical map, thanks to technology.

14

In simple terms, the bright blue of the background is electronically "keyed" out and replaced by a weather map or whatever else you want. The way we know what we're pointing at is by watching ourselves on TVs set to either side of the wall and a TV picture shown to us on the teleprompter over the lens of the camera. Without these, we'd be blind. Ever notice how some weather people never seem to look back at what they're pointing at, but somehow manage to find Kansas anyway? That's because they're just watching themselves on television. To maintain the illusion, you must turn to look at the recessed monitors. That way, you appear to be looking at this nonexistent map.

Anyone who's visited a TV studio to watch a weather segment knows it's kind of strange to see in person. But when I'm actually standing out there, there are three things I have to keep in mind. One, everything's backwards. It's like looking into a mirror. Two, the background maps never change size, even if the camera zooms in. However, if I step toward the camera, I can look huge. If I step back, I will appear to shrink. Third, and this is very important, **never wear chromakey blue**! If I do, I'll vanish. And all the folks at home will see is my floating head and hands bobbing along in front of the map. Fortunately, I don't have any suits that color, but before each show, the camera must be adjusted for the day's wardrobe so that I don't "key out."

Note: Chromakey is **BIG** in the special effects business. That's how they make Superman fly in the movies. The actor is suspended, cape and all, in front of a chromakey wall. Aerial photographs of clouds and buildings flying past are then "keyed" in behind the actor. By the way, an obvious blue or green halo around an actor, is a sign of a "bad key."

BLUE SKY

Nice day, right? Beautiful blue skies, winter or summer, seem to brighten our moods. But have you ever wondered why the sky is blue? No? Well, I'm going to tell you anyway.

The light that reaches the Earth from the Sun actually contains all the colors in the rainbow. The color we see depends on the way we perceive it as well as the way in which the incoming sunlight is scattered by the atmosphere. Even though you can't see it, for the most part, our air is chock full of tiny little particles like dust, water, and various gases. Each of these acts like a roadblock to the incoming sunlight.

The result is that light is scattered around. How much depends on the size of the roadblock and the wavelength of the light. Just like in a rainbow, blue is on one side of the spectrum, red is at the other. Since the blue waves are much shorter, they are scattered better. As a result, the sky **looks** blue.

But what about those beautiful yellow and red sunrises and sunsets, you ask? Same principle. As the sun gets near the horizon, at dawn or dusk, the shorter blue waves are finally scattered away. At this point, since the light is coming in at such an angle and is passing through so much more atmosphere, only the longer red and yellow waves last to reach the eye. And when you have clouds in the sky, they can pick up these colors creating breathtaking, though short-lived, sunsets.

Not to get too carried away, but let's take this one step further. What would you see if you were to blast off into orbit aboard a space shuttle? Well, there's less and less atmosphere and fewer and fewer roadblocks as you go up. So eventually, there's no scattering at all. The result: the sky gets darker and darker until it turns completely black.

BOW ECHO

These can be a real cause for concern when we spot them on Doppler radar. A bow echo is a classic radar signature for potentially severe thunderstorms, especially the kind that produce damaging winds. These strong lines of storms bend outward, taking the shape of a bow. Bow echoes tend to be most common during Ohio's stormy spring and summer months from April to August.

BUZZARDS OF HINCKLEY

Sure, you've got your equinoxes and your ground hogs, but nothing truly says spring better than a bunch of big, ugly, migratory birds and the Ohio town that claims them.

As the story goes, just like Capistrano and the proverbial trek made by its swallows, the little town of Hinckley in Medina County claims the annual return of the buzzards on the 15th of March, just in time for the town's big pancake and sausage breakfast. (Nice of them to be so punctual.)

The buzzards, which are actually turkey vultures, aren't much to look at and have some downright nasty habits. But after a long, cold winter, they're a sure sign that spring is just around the corner. They also make a good 20-second piece of weather video on the evening news!

CELSIUS

Celsius is the temperature scale that most of the rest of the world uses! *I guess we're just stubborn when it comes to all things metric.* Actually, the Celsius temperature scale would be much easier to work with. Water freezes at zero degrees Celsius (instead of 32 degrees Fahrenheit) and boils at 100 degrees Celsius (instead of 212 degrees Fahrenheit). The problem is, if you're used to Fahrenheit, the other seems strange and alien. Celsius is, however, the internationally used scale. *Old habits die hard!*

The Celsius scale has been around for a long, long time. It was invented by Anders Celsius, a Swedish astronomer, in 1742. (see **Fahrenheit** for a conversion table)

CENTER OF SCIENCE AND INDUSTRY (COSI)
Columbus, Ohio

The Center of Science and Industry (COSI) in Columbus, Ohio, is a tremendous scientific resource for young and old alike. Better still, it's a great place to play and learn all at the same time. Located down by the Scioto River in the capital city, COSI explores and explains all manner of things scientific, biological, and environmental... including the weather and the Earth.

Going hand in hand are exhibits about the oceans and "The Ocean Above, Our Global Weather." The "Ocean Above" features videotapes of me explaining everything from Doppler Radar to El Niño and Global Warming. We also have an operating, live weather station which displays current readings of pressure, temperature, wind speed, etc., at COSI as well as "Live, Dual Doppler 10 Radar."

There are also a variety of daily live shows in which we demonstrate how to make a cloud indoors and what happens when you mix the raw elements of the atmosphere together. There is also a show that simulates the power of a tornado or hurricane by shooting a pencil through blocks of wood.

The "Ocean Above, Our Global Weather" is hands on and fun-filled. What's more, I had a great time working with those fine folks at COSI putting it all together. The exhibit, which also features a simulated tornado, has been extremely popular with local school groups looking to enhance their understanding of this complicated and interconnected environment in which we live.

CHEIMAPHOBIA

Believe it or not, there's a name for the fear of cold temperatures, and it's not "Minnesotaphobia." (They have a name for everything, don't they?) Cheimaphobia would not be a good thing to have during a central Ohio winter. In fact, if you had it, you would have been downright terrified during the winter of 1994, when January temperatures fell to record levels all across the Buckeye state.

While weather preferences are a very personal and individual thing, research indicates that most folks can tolerate heat better than cold. (I am not one of these folks.)

CINCINNATI

The "Queen City," nestled along the mighty Ohio River in southwestern Ohio is home to the Reds and the Bengals. It's not that far from Columbus, but certain geographic features make for some subtle differences in the weather. It's a little warmer, a little more rainy, and a little less snowy. The Ohio River  Valley has an impact. Storm systems tend to roll up the valley moving southwest to northeast, bringing some of that summer rain. The city is also surrounded by scenic rolling hills.

Like Columbus, Cincinnati has moderately cold, cloudy winters. Summers can also be kind of warm. On average there are twenty-three 90-degree days each year. And one year in three, the mercury hits the century mark! The last frost usually hits around mid-April, while the first frost of the season tends to occur in late October. By the way, the all-time record high was 109°F in July of 1934.

FYI: The name Cincinnati was chosen to honor an organization of Revolutionary War veterans who called themselves the Society of the Cincinnati.

Average Temperature (in degrees Fahrenheit) and Precipitation (in inches) for Cincinnati, Ohio

(Elevation: 869 feet)

Month	Temperature High	Low	Precipitation	Snowfall
January	37	20	2.59	7
February	41	23	2.69	5
March	53	33	4.24	4
April	64	42	3.75	1
May	74	52	4.28	Trace
June	80	58	3.84	0
July	86	65	4.24	Are you kidding?
August	84	63	3.35	0
September	78	57	2.88	0
October	66	44	2.86	Trace
November	53	35	3.46	2
December	42	25	3.15	4

source: National Weather Service

CLEAR

Clear describes a sky condition as well as the way in which we try to make a forecast. By definition, a clear sky has no clouds. Clear skies allow for more solar heating during the day and more cooling at night. Have you heard the expression "on a clear day you can see forever?" Well, that's not quite true. Even clear days have their limits. If the air is perfectly clear (no dust or pollution), you're still limited to about 200 miles of visibility, barring any large obstacles like buildings.

CLEVELAND

Life, and the weather, is different up on the shores of Lake Erie. In fact, the lake is the major force in Cleveland's weather. That's not too hard to understand given that water makes up 31 miles of the city's shoreline! Northerly winds blowing off the lake help keep the city a little cooler in the summer and a little milder in the winter. Thunderstorms are common from April through August, and snow is VERY common in the winter, to the tune of about 55 inches each year. To be fair, though, snowfall varies greatly from year to year. How's this for an example? The record 24-hour snowfall in Cleveland is 17.4 inches, which occurred November 10–11, 1913. The record monthly snowfall, coincidentally, was during the month of the Great Blizzard, January, 1978. The grand total was 42.8 inches of snow… in ONE MONTH! Oddly enough, despite the snowfall extremes, the average precipitation in Cleveland is slightly less than either Columbus or Cincinnati.

FYI: Cleveland, Ohio, was named for General Moses Cleaveland, who founded it back in 1796. The spelling changed when some map-makers omitted the first "a" in the general's name. Local newspapers adopted the present spelling in 1832.

Average Temperature (in degrees Fahrenheit) and Precipitation (in inches) for Cleveland, Ohio

(Elevation: 869 feet)

Month	Temperature High	Low	Precipitation	Snowfall
January	32	18	1.04	13
February	35	19	2.19	12
March	46	28	2.91	10
April	58	37	3.14	2
May	69	47	3.49	Trace
June	78	57	3.70	0
July	82	61	3.40	0
August	80	60	3.44	0
September	74	54	3.44	0
October	62	43	2.54	1
November	50	35	3.17	5
December	37	24	3.09	12

source: National Weather Service

CLIMATE

Every region of the world has one. And, while some climates are "better" than others, they're something we must all adjust to since they represent the long-term tendencies of the weather. Here's an easy way to remember it: the weather is what's actually happening, but climate is what's supposed to happen. (see **Normal**)

Not to be outdone by meteorology, climate has a science of its own... climatology. Climatology is, for all intents and purposes, weather history. More precisely, State of Ohio Climatologist, Dr. Jeff Rogers, says, "climate is the average of weather."

Forecasts (i.e., meteorology) are based upon this history. Without good and long-term climatology, there would be no forecasting as we know it. Forecasting is based upon things that have happened before and, therefore, might very well happen again. We learn from our mistakes, hopefully, and move on.

Technically speaking, Ohio's climate is "continental," with moderate extremes of temperature and precipitation.

For the entire Buckeye state, the average annual temperature is 50°F. But different parts of the state do experience local influences, such as the lake-effect snow in the snow belt.

On the other hand, the rolling hills of southeast Ohio, besides providing some lovely scenery, offer the added benefit of some protection from Ohio's most violent storm: the tornado. Fewer tornadoes occur here than in central Ohio, due to the influences of hilly terrain upon storm systems. But keep in mind, as weather phenomena go, there are NO absolutes or guarantees. (see **Tornado**)

CLOUDS

Clouds are a part of every weather forecast. We use time-lapse satellite photography to show exactly where they are and to predict how soon they'll be here. We tell you when to expect them, how many there will be and, most importantly, when they'll go away again. Ohio is **not** the sunniest of states. Therefore, clouds are very important to the forecast. The amount and type of clouds can drastically impact our moods, as well as the forecasted high and low for the day.

Since we have so many, it's probably a good idea to take a look at where they come from and why. Clouds form when air cools to the point that the water vapor in the air condenses. The temperature at which this occurs is called the dew point. There are three basic ways that clouds form.

Ways Clouds Form

1. Heating during the day causes warm, moist air to rise. The air then cools as it rises, until it reaches the dew point temperature. At this level, the moisture condenses, forming a cloud.

2. Fronts, caused by different temperature air masses, cause warmer air to rise as it is undercut by the heavier cold air. Again, when it hits the condensation level, clouds form.

3. Geographic features, like mountains, deflect air upwards until it condenses.

Clouds also come in three basic varieties: high, middle, and low clouds. The most common types of low clouds are the puffy ones (cumulus and cumulonimbus) and the layered ones (stratus and stratocumulus and nimbostratus), which are basically stratus clouds from which rain may fall. Of the middle variety, altocumulus, altostratus, and nimbostratus are most common. Cirrus, cirrostratus, and cirrocumulus, the primary high clouds, are mostly made of ice as opposed to water.

Clouds can be used in forecasting. Farmers, pilots, even balloonists are especially good at this. For example, advancing feathery-looking cirrus clouds often signal that a front is approaching and that rain can be expected within 24 hours. A blue or gray sheet of altostratus clouds can give the sky a frosted appearance and often means rain in 6–12 hours.

Cloud Experiment:

To make your own cloud, you'll need a large glass jar, some hot water, a small metal baking pan and some ice. Pour about an inch of hot water into the bottom of the empty jar. Then, put some ice cubes onto the small baking tray and place it on top of the jar. As the warm air in the jar rises, it will be cooled by the ice. The water vapor will condense, forming a cloud.

COFFEE

Can a cup of coffee help forecast the weather? It sure helps me! But that's beside the point. According to folk-lore, the bubbles in your coffee can actually help to predict the weather. Supposedly, if coffee bubbles in the center

Can a cup of coffee help forecast the weather?

of your cup, there will be fair weather. If the bubbles gather around the sides of the cup, you'd better dig out your umbrella. Finally, if the bubbles appear randomly scattered, you're in for changeable weather. I wonder if that holds true for regular and decaf? That also brings up a question: will several cups make my forecasts a latte better?

COLDS & FLU

"Don't go out, dear. You'll catch your death of cold." Sure. We've all heard it. But can the weather actually cause a cold? Like so many things, if we say it enough, it must be true. Right? WRONG. Germs cause colds. Bottom line: the weather cannot create the germs that cause colds. However, changes in the weather **can** affect your body's resistance to these germs.

How is this possible? Well, if your body undergoes a sudden, deep chilling, it can apparently have an impact on the mucous membranes in the upper respiratory tract, weakening them, thereby providing a perfect breeding ground for the germs that actually do cause colds. Of course, I don't want to make this a medical reference book, but I thought it was worth mentioning. Still, it just so happens that my initials are M.D.

COLUMBUS

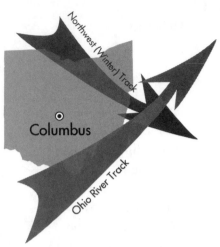

Weather is like real estate. It's location, location, location! By definition, Columbus means "wait five minutes and it'll change." And it will never be known as *Sunshine City!* Why? Well, Columbus is between a couple of major weather tracks. For example, we're frequently invaded by air masses from central and northwestern Canada. (Don't worry. These invading air masses are generally friendly, though they can give us the cold shoulder from time to time.) Meanwhile, a lot of our moisture, especially during the summer months, comes all the way from the Gulf of Mexico.

On average, the city's first freeze occurs in very late October, while the last freeze usually hits about mid-April. But as anyone living in the "vicinity" knows, there's quite a bit of variation across the suburbs and surroundings. The average snowfall is about 28 inches, while total yearly moisture is almost 38 inches. If you break it down further, we average about 56 days with snow (not to be confused with school snow days), 136 wet days, and 40 days with thunderstorms. We're also in a fog about 158 days each year.

Columbus' all-time record high was 106°F in July 1936, while the all-time record low was a bone-chilling -22°F degrees in January of 1994. The record snowfall was 12.3 inches on April 4, 1987. The worst (best?) month for snow was the now-infamous January 1978, the month of the Great Blizzard. The record 24-hour rainfall was a whopping 5.16 inches on July 12–13, 1992. (That one was a drought-buster.)

FYI: The name Columbus was chosen to honor the faith in the future, the courage and the persistence of Christopher Columbus.

Average Temperature (in degrees Fahrenheit) and Precipitation (in inches) for Columbus, Ohio

(Elevation: 813 feet)

Month	Temperature High	Low	Precipitation	Snowfall
January	34	19	2.18	8
February	38	21	2.24	6
March	51	31	3.27	5
April	62	40	3.21	1
May	72	50	3.93	Trace
June	80	58	4.04	0
July	84	63	4.31	Are you kidding?
August	82	61	3.72	0
September	76	55	2.96	0
October	65	43	2.15	Trace
November	51	34	3.22	2
December	39	25	2.86	5

source: National Weather Service

COMPUTERS

Let's be honest. We could not do what we do without computers. We use weather computers to animate satellite and radar pictures, to zoom through the clouds in a "fly-by," to draw on the various maps of Ohio and the United States, and to put those maps on TV. But even before all that happens, we rely on computers to help forecast the weather.

All the observations that are taken by weather instruments around the country, from thermometers to weather balloons, are fed into super-computers at a place called the National Centers for Environmental Prediction (NCEP) in Washington, D.C. There, mighty mechanical minds sift through the data and put it into maps that show the current state of the weather as well as what's expected to happen over the next 12, 24, 36, 48 hours, etc. These maps are then sent to meteorologists all over the country. The funny thing is, we all basically look at the **same** data, but still come up with **different** conclusions!

Interpreting (decoding) all this information is what forecasting is all about. It's the meteorologist's job to use his or her own background and experience to decide whether the computers are right or wrong.

CRAWLS

Beep! Beep! Beep! These are the little messages that run along the top or bottom of your TV screen. (Usually during your favorite show.) Contrary to popular opinion, a crawl is not meant to strike fear into the hearts of the unsuspecting public. They are merely there to inform you of everything from stormy weather to school closings to lottery numbers. It's a way of getting a message, which we think is important, to the viewer **without** interrupting programming. Crawls seem to fall under the category of "love 'em or hate 'em." Little storm symbols or eye-straining county maps are variations on that same basic theme.

CRITICISM

Criticism comes with the territory, baby. And as someone told me early in my career, you can't be too thin-skinned AND be a meteorologist… especially one that makes his living in front of the camera!

Besides politicians, and possibly lawyers, is there another group of professionals that gets lambasted more in editorial cartoons than those of us in the weather biz?

"Chaos Theory" better explains the complex vertical and horizontal properties of our weather than any of our current mathematical models. It's doubtful that weather forecasts will ever be perfect, but research continues. Until then, there's a reasonable probability (chance) that our forecasts, especially the extended ones, will be at least partly wrong, with scattered errors and intermittent glitches on occasion. (see **Forecasting**)

CRYING WOLF

If you'll excuse the expression, this is the *bane* of our existence. I try to guard against this. For one thing, I don't panic easily. Keep in mind, extreme weather events like big winter storms and devastating tornado outbreaks are the **exception** rather than the **rule**. Still, the potential is always there. That's why you see so many watches, warnings, and advisories. These are guidelines… little reminders to be careful.

The reaction to all these "little reminders" varies greatly. Some people would rather not be bothered at all. After all "weather happens." Others say we still don't give enough warning. Even so, new technology gives us a little more of an edge every day. Still, our own judgment and experience as forecasters play a major role in the calls we make.

Just as an example, weather charts forecast moisture, either rain or snow, as a water equivalent. Keep in mind that the water equivalent for rain versus snow is roughly 10-to-1 for your basic "wet snow." Now, the forecasting models we use may say that we're expecting 1.4 inches of moisture from what appears to be a pretty strong storm. Should I forecast 14 inches of snow? Most of the time no, since this is an exceedingly rare event in central Ohio. Again, that's where experience and common sense factor in. If you call for 14 inches of snow, as the chart may indicate, the odds really aren't in your favor. It's a judgment call. On one hand, you don't want to minimize the obvious potential… but on the other hand, if you cry wolf too often, who's going to listen any more?

CUMULONIMBUS CLOUDS

The big boomers! They're kind of like a cumulus cloud's big brother. These are thunderstorm clouds, from the Latin words meaning "piled up" and "rain." Actually, that's pretty descriptive since these are towering white clouds that stretch high into the sky, often with flattened "anvil" shaped tops. Cumulonimbus clouds go so high that they always contain ice crystals. They flatten out when they hit the bottom of the stratosphere. Anvil tops and black bottoms are a sure sign of rain and storms to come. They are known for producing thunder and lightning, heavy rain, strong winds and downdrafts, hail, and even tornadoes. (see **Anvil**)

CUMULUS CLOUDS

These are among the most common *fair weather* clouds. They're white and fluffy and kind of look like floating pieces of cauliflower. These are the ones that, as you're lying on your back on a summer afternoon, you look up and say, "that one looks like an elephant." "That one looks like Mt. Rushmore."

Cumulus means "piled up" in Latin. **Puffy.** They tend to pop up in the afternoon as warm air rises and condenses. That's what clouds are, you know, condensed water vapor. If you want to get technical, there are many types of cumulus clouds.

- Cumulus Congestus: "congested" cumulus clouds that swell forming towers and off-shoots (especially puffy clouds).
- Cumulus Humilis: "humble" or "lowly" cumulus clouds.
- Cumulus Fractus: "broken" cumulus clouds.
- Cumulus Lenticularis: "lens-shaped" cumulus clouds, usually mid-level cumulus.
- Cumulus Castellanus: "turreted" altocumulus or cirrocumulus clouds.

Folklore: "Mountains in the morning, fountains in the evening."

These are cirrus clouds, higher up.

CYCLONE

Remember the terrible twister in the *Wizard of Oz*? "Toto, it's a cyclone!" Well, yes and no. Cyclone is a versatile term in meteorology. And lots of things are cyclones. A cyclone is an organized area of low pressure, meaning the air rotates in a counter-clockwise fashion. (In the Northern Hemisphere.) In some parts of the world, a cyclone refers to a tropical storm or hurricane. And, yes, it was once a common term for a tornado.

DAYTON

Dayton is near the center of the Miami River Valley. A moderate climate helps make the Miami Valley a rich agricultural area. Humidity in the valley remains fairly high year 'round. Temperature extremes don't last long, and polar air flowing across the Great Lakes makes for cloudy winters, just like Columbus.

FYI: Although first called Cabintown, the name was changed to Dayton after John Dayton who was one of the purchasers of the land.

DEGREE DAY

This is a little understood term that gets most of its use from folks in the heating and cooling industry. It's a measure of the departure of the average daily temperature from a given standard. There's one Heating Degree Day for each degree below 65°F. This is an indicator of your fuel consumption (and your heating bill).

A Cooling Degree Day, on the other hand, represents each degree above 75°F. Again, the more cooling degree days, the bigger your air conditioning bill. In both cases, it's all about comfort and cost.

Average Temperature (in degrees Fahrenheit) and Precipitation (in inches) for Dayton, Ohio

(Elevation: 995 feet)

Month	Temperature High	Low	Precipitation	Snowfall
January	34	18	2.13	8
February	33	21	2.17	6
March	50	31	3.42	5
April	62	41	3.46	1
May	73	51	3.88	Trace
June	82	59	3.82	0
July	85	63	3.54	0
August	83	61	3.20	0
September	77	55	2.54	0
October	65	44	2.48	Trace
November	51	34	3.07	2
December	39	24	2.93	6

source: National Weather Service

DEPRESSION

That's what sets in when I said it would be beautiful on Saturday… only to wake up to the sound of raindrops beating on the window. But that's another story. On a weather map, a depression is an area of low pressure. From the right angle, it looks like a dip or a depressed area on a pressure chart, hence the name.

When you hear this term at home, it's usually attached to a word like tropical, as in tropical depression. This is the baby brother of a hurricane. (see **Hurricane**)

DEW

Dew is the moisture that forms on the grass in the morning on cloud-free, clear nights with little or no wind. (see **Dew Point**)

Folklore: Dew on the grass, rain won't come to pass.

DEW POINT

We don't talk about it much on the evening news, but dew point is actually a very important weather term. The dew point is a measure of humidity. It is also the temperature where dew forms, since this is the temperature where the air can't hold any more moisture. The air temperature and the dew point temperature are used to calculate relative humidity, which is expressed as a percentage. (This is the one you hear about on the news.) If the temperature and the dew point are the same, the relative humidity is 100%.

This usually occurs in the morning, if at all, about the time the morning low hits. That's why the grass will be wet in the morning, even when it hasn't rained overnight and why you'll have a soggy newspaper if it's been lying in the grass. By the way, if this temperature is below freezing, we call it the frost point.

DOG DAYS OF SUMMER

What is it about animals and the weather? Did you ever notice how our pets and other critters creep into everyday conversations about the weather? For example, "It's raining cats and dogs out there!" And what's all this about March coming in like a lion and going out like a lamb? Or is it in like a lamb, out like a lion? Oh… and don't forget about Groundhog Day! (Hey, they even made a movie about that.)

But one of the most popular expressions rolls around every year, just when you think the long, hot summer is never going to end: the dog days of summer. What are the dog days of summer? And how did they become the dog days? And how is a "dog day" different than any other kind of day? Tough questions, eh?

I suppose it could mean that we've all gotten "dog tired" of being so hot all the time. We certainly seem to have our fair share of those days every year. Or does it refer to those lazy, hazy, late summer days when all you feel like doing is lying out in the sun like Ol' Spot? Actually, some say the expression dates all the way back to the ancient Greeks and Romans who blamed the late summer swelter on the heat radiating from the stars at night.

For most of the continental United States, including Ohio, one of the hottest times of the year is the period from mid-July until late August when, coincidentally, the Dog Star, Sirius, rises just before sunrise. Hey, maybe the Dog Star is the culprit behind this late summer sizzle. NOT! These days are typically hot, not because of starlight, but because the energy we receive from the Sun is still greater than the energy the Earth radiates back into space. It's also the time of year when the northern jet stream retreats northward into Canada, and we tend to be influenced by the subtropical jet stream that brings in warm, humid air from the Gulf of Mexico.

When the "dog days" hit, it also means that fall, the autumnal equinox, is just around the corner. *Doggone it!* Of course, it also means a return to cool nights, "good sleeping weather," and football season! Of course, when it comes to the changing of the seasons, everyone has a favorite. And as changeable as the weather tends to be in Ohio, it's probably best if we just take it as it comes. In other words, don't take it all so Sirius-ly.

DOPPLER RADAR

As a freight train approaches a crossing, it blows its whistle. As the train approaches, the pitch of the shrill whistle seems to rise. As the train rolls past, the pitch falls. In truth, however, the pitch never changes, only the way we perceive it because of how the train is moving. This is called the Doppler effect, named after a man named J. Christian Doppler (1803-1853), an Austrian physicist.

WBNS 10TV in Columbus had the first and only Doppler radar in central Ohio for years. These days, we actually have two. I'm sure you know because we talk about it ALL the time. But have you ever wondered what the difference is between a Doppler radar and a regular radar? If conventional radar looks for rain and snow, what does Doppler radar look for? Dopplers?

Sure, Doppler radars show rain, snow, and thunderstorms, but they actually see much more. Doppler radars let meteorologists look inside thunderstorms, by computing wind speed and direction. What are we looking for? We're looking for winds moving in opposite directions that may actually start rotating. This spinning often leads to the formation of tornadoes. Doppler radars give forecasters valuable lead-time for predicting where severe storms may develop.

The National Weather Service has now taken the Doppler principle one step further. They have installed NEXRADs, or Next Generation Doppler Radars, in Wilmington, Ohio, down in the southwestern part of the state, and in Cleveland. These powerful new radars will keep an eye on the weather statewide. In fact, they are so sophisticated that tornado warnings will be issued based on radar reports rather than waiting for law enforcement or the public to phone in a sighting.

Between the NEXRADs and 10TV's exclusive Dual Doppler radars, we have you covered Ohio!

Note: When judging a TV station's Doppler Radar, be sure it's "live" Doppler radar. That means you're seeing a real-time image of what's going on now. Some stations and cable channels display what amounts to a tape-delayed image. Do you remember the old advertising slogan "Is it Live, or is it Memorex®?" This is far more important in the context of radar imagery.

DOWNBURST

A downburst is a very strong downdraft from a severe thunderstorm. These cold winds hit the ground, fanning out, causing damage that, at times, can resemble the devastation caused by a tornado. When you go out to the damage scene, following a downburst, you often find a very well-defined damage path. In one case, I saw one house completely flattened, but the house next door was completely untouched... right down to the glass bottles and knick-knacks sitting on the front porch.

In many ways, the sound from the rush of air can mimic the so-called "freight train" noise of a tornado. It's splitting hairs, but sometimes the only way to tell the difference between damage caused by a tornado and damage caused by a downburst is to do an after-the-fact inspection. National Weather Service investigators go to the scene looking for signs of twisting that indicate that the storm was rotating (a tornado).

A smaller scale, but equally damaging, downdraft is often referred to as a microburst. By definition, a microburst would be confined to an area of 2.5 miles or less and would last less than 5 minutes.

DRIZZLE

Here's a dreary one. What is it that will leave your newspaper soggy in the morning, will give you a bad hair day, makes it especially tough to find the right interval setting on your windshield wipers, and yet hardly amounts to anything when it comes to watering your lawn or filling up the ol' rain gauge? One word. Drizzle.

Drizzle typically falls from layered stratus type clouds. In fact, drizzle is the condition that occurs when the drops are just barely big enough to fall at all. So, in a nutshell, drizzle is a kind of precipitation made up of tiny water droplets. (Less than 0.02 inches to be exact. The drops also fall close together.) If drizzle falls into colder air, so that it freezes on contact with other surfaces, it's called freezing drizzle. Freezing drizzle is a nasty and deceptive weather condition, since it seems so harmless if you were to just hold out your hand. But it will quickly ice up your windows, as well as streets and sidewalks, making any kind of safe travel extremely difficult.

By the way, have you ever been caught in a "blinding drizzle?" The two terms sound like they don't go together... and they don't. But there are "degrees of drizzle." Oh? You bet! The intensity of drizzle is based on visibility. Light drizzle implies visibility of more than $1/2$ mile. Moderate drizzle means visibility is between $1/4$ to $1/2$ mile. Heavy drizzle has visibility less than $1/4$ mile. My colleague Angela Pace is partial to the term "raging drizzle." (see **Rain**)

DROUGHT

A drought is a particularly harsh dry spell that can have a devastating impact on farming, livestock, the economy, and people. Water is essential for life. Serious water shortages, such as those which occur during a drought, can range from inconvenient to life threatening.

A drought happens when the air flow prevents needed moisture from reaching an area for a prolonged period of time. This can occur when "blocking" areas of high pressure set up, like an omega block, which keep showers and storms from moving west to east as they normally would. What constitutes a drought in one area of the country, may not be considered a drought in another. But generally, you're talking about a period of time of at least 2–3 weeks, with 30 percent or less of the usual moisture. (see **Omega Block**)

When we slip into a drought, you'll hear those of us on the news referring to something called the Palmer Drought Severity Index. The index was developed by National Weather Service meteorologist Wayne Palmer back in the 1950s. It's a simple case of supply and demand. Rainfall and soil moisture make up the supply side of the equation, while a combination of soil moisture, evaporation, and runoff to maintain stream, river, lake, and reservoir levels make up the demand side. A water-balance ratio is then determined. This ratio is broken down into:

1. Moist
2. Near Normal
3. Moderate Drought
4. Severe Drought
5. Extreme Drought

The drought index also goes as far as expressing the amount of moisture needed to end the drought. In addition to the Palmer Index, there's also a short-term Crop Moisture Index, which is computed weekly. It's a measure of whether growing crops had enough moisture over the previous week. In any case, a long-lasting drought can have a devastating effect on a region's people and economy.

DUST

Guess what? Dust isn't all bad! In fact, dust plays an important role in our weather. First, there are many kinds of dust in the air. There's dust from car exhaust, bare fields and erosion, fires, even volcanoes. You can also find airborne salts picked up from the oceans, plant pollens, even mold spores.

What does any of this actually have to do with the weather? Well, all these tiny particles give the water in the air something to hold on to. Tiny droplets form as the water vapor clings to these even tinier particles. These droplets can then grow by running into each other and forming bigger droplets or raindrops. Eventually, the drop grows to the point where it's too heavy to keep floating in the cloud, so it falls to the Earth as rain. It's the same basic process during the winter, except that ice crystals gather around the tiny dust particles and form snowflakes.

EARTHQUAKES

I'm neither a geologist nor a seismologist, but as a "science guy," I always end up fielding questions whenever the Earth shakes. Luckily, it doesn't shake much in Ohio. And when it does, it doesn't shake too badly, at least not by California standards. First of all, no one has ever died from an Ohio quake. What's more, there's not a whole lot o' shakin' goin' on in central Ohio. No quake has ever been centered in Franklin, Union, Madison, Pickaway, Fairfield, or Licking counties.

Most of Ohio's underground quakes aren't even felt on the surface. Ohio's earthquake zone runs along a rift near the Shelby County town of Anna. And surprise, surprise… the Anna arc is the second most active earthquake zone east of the Mississippi! Only the New Madrid Fault produces more quakes. But unlike California quakes, which result from faults at or near the surface, Ohio's faults are deeply buried and not well understood.

Ohio's biggest quake, a 5.5 on the Richter scale near Anna on March 9, 1937, was dubbed the "Buckeye Biggie." Ohio's other top tremors occurred near Anna, another 5.0 just a week earlier, a 5.0 at Painesville in 1986, a 4.8 in Lima way back in 1884, and a 4.6 at St. Marys in 1986. Of course, things were different a billion years ago when Ohio was at the edge of the North American plate. Tremendous collisions back then created large faults and built mountains. Today, the mountains are long gone, and the faults are deeply buried and mostly forgotten.

Note: The Richter Magnitude Scale, widely used to measure the intensity of earthquakes, was designed by an Ohioan, Charles F. Richter back in 1935 while working for the California Institute of Technology.

ELEVATION

Changing elevations can have a major impact on a forecast both in terms of temperature and precipitation. What would fall as rain at the warmer low levels of our atmosphere could very well be snow at a slightly higher (and generally cooler) elevation. Fortunately, for me that is, elevation isn't a big issue here in Ohio. This is especially true for the flat lands of central Ohio.

Just to give you an idea, Ohio's low point (geographically speaking, since I'm making no value judgements here) is at the junction of the Miami and Ohio Rivers in Hamilton County in southwestern Ohio. The elevation there is just 430 feet above sea level. By contrast, the elevation in Columbus is 813 feet. Mansfield stands a comparatively towering 1295 feet above sea level. But the state's high point is Campbell Hill in Logan County, just to the southeast of Bellefontaine… a whopping 1550 feet! Though it's only part of the reason, both these high points get considerably more winter snowfall than the Columbus area.

EL NIÑO

El Niño pays a visit to the United States every now and then, and the result can be a rather dramatic impact on the weather. Who is this El Niño? Isn't that Zorro's old sidekick? He must be pretty old by now! Or is he some nasty South American dictator? To the contrary, El Niño means "the child," because it's a phenomenon that typically occurs around Christmas time every two to five years.

El Niño begins when warm ocean water flows northward out of the tropical Pacific Ocean and up along the west coast of the United States. This surge of warm water affects the air it comes into contact with, thereby influencing temperature, wind, and precipitation nationwide. Experts have blamed everything from flooding and mudslides to drought on El Niño.

During El Niño years, the east and west coasts tend to experience particularly stormy weather. The Ohio Valley, historically speaking, tends to get away with a mild winter and near normal precipitation. The year after an El Niño is a completely different story. On the plus side, El Niño years tend to be quiet ones in terms of hurricanes and tropical storms. But here in the United States, the impact of El Niño, one year later, can be felt coast to coast.

The year following El Niño tends to bring dry weather to the Ohio Valley during the summer and cold and snowy winters across the entire Midwest. We saw this happen back in 1984 when cities across the Midwest set snowfall records and suffered through repeated blasts of cold, arctic air.

El Niño of 1997-98 brought some of the mildest winter weather in Ohio history. Of course, since weather patterns tend to be cyclical, you have to take the good with the bad. (see **La Niña**)

EQUINOX

Equinoxes occur twice a year and represent the astronomical beginnings of spring and fall. They're also the time when days and nights around the world are equal. The vernal equinox (spring) falls on or about March 20th, while the autumnal equinox (fall) occurs on or about September 22nd.

The reason for seasons in the first place is that our planet is tilted. The Earth's axis always points toward the North Star, an angle of 23 $^1/_2$ degrees. (see **Solstice**)

EVAPORATION

Another key process for heat and moisture exchange in the atmosphere, it's the conversion of water from a liquid into a gas. As part of the water cycle, water is transferred from the surface to the atmosphere through evaporation. This water may later condense and fall back into the rivers and oceans as rain. Condensation is the conversion of water from a gas into a liquid.

EXTREMES

Let's be honest, as bitter as it feels some days in the dead of winter, and as oppressively humid as it is during the dog days of summer, Ohio's weather extremes, relatively speaking, are not that extreme. Still, we do have quite a bit of... variety.

Ohio's record low was a bone-chilling -39°F in Milligan way back on the 10th of February, 1899. The all-time record high was a mere 152 degrees warmer than that! Ohio's record high was 113°F in Gallipolis on the 21st of July, 1934.

How 'bout the snowiest storm ever? You don't have to go too far back for that one. The city of Chardon, in Northeast Ohio (see **Snow Belt**), got buried by 73 inches of snow in November of 1996. By the way, Chardon once picked up 161.5 inches of snow... in a single winter, back in 1959–1960. (I'm sure shovel sales are quite good in Chardon.)

Here's another good one. The heaviest one hour rainfall was 3.58 inches in Toledo on the 16th of August, 1920. Meanwhile, Sandusky holds the 24-hour rainfall record for Ohio with a torrential 10.51 inches on July 12, 1966. (OK, I take that "extreme" thing back.)

FAHRENHEIT

It's our way of measuring the temperature, and we're sticking to it! Obviously, we don't care much that most of the rest of the world has gone metric. Of course, we meteorologists use Celsius in our work, but it's never really caught on with the American public... even though it's easier to use.

Invented by Gabriel Fahrenheit in 1714, the Fahrenheit temperature scale says water freezes at 32 degrees. That's the part most of us know. On the Celsius scale, water freezes at zero degrees. To convert from Celsius to Fahrenheit, multiply the temperature by 1.8 and add 32 degrees (or see the easy chart below).

Fahrenheit/Celsius Conversion Table		
Fahrenheit		**Celsius**
212°	water boils	100°
194°		90°
176°		80°
158°		70°
140°		60°
122°		50°
104°		40°
86°		30°
68°	average room temperature	20°
50°		10°
32°	water freezes	0°

FAIR WEATHER

To me, this is an almost worthless term. Why? Because it really doesn't hold much meaning for the average viewer. OK, it kind of means… nice. But how nice? Oh sure, we all like to use it during "fair" season. Especially during the run of the Ohio State Fair. "Will we see fair skies for the fair? A fairly fair fair forecast, coming up." Ughhh!

How is fair different than clear? Well, for one thing, fair is less clear than clear. Fair implies that there are some clouds. So why not say partly cloudy? The word fair seems to turn up most often in the extended (3–5 day) forecast. "Fair skies through the period." Really, all that means is that it looks like a rain free period, not to be confused with "sunny skies all week."

By definition, fair means few or no clouds below 12,000 feet with no significant weather and/or obstructions to visibility. In truth, though, there's very little difference between fair and partly cloudy skies. To be fair, fair is a fairly nice weather condition in which nothing extreme is happening.

FALL COLOR

Most years, you can count on the Buckeye state for gorgeous fall color. But would you believe me if I told you that those beautiful shades of red, amber, yellow, and orange are in the leaves year 'round? Well, it's true. You just can't see them because of the green.

During the growing season, the green color comes from a pigment called chlorophyll. Through a process called photosynthesis, chlorophyll captures the Sun's energy and converts it into sugars that help trees grow. That's no problem in the summer. But as days grow short and nights grow cold during the fall, this process slows down, and those deep greens start to fade. That's when fall color, which is always there, starts to show through. The yellows, browns, and oranges come from pigments called carotenoids. Reds, purples, and their blends come from anthocyanins, which begin to develop in sap cells by late summer.

How vibrant the shades of autumn turn out to be depends on the amount of rainfall during the year as well as a combination of fall sunshine and cool nights. This is yet another one of those things that's totally weather dependent. Fall color updates are available each year through 1-800-BUCKEYE via the Ohio Department of Natural Resource's Fall Color Hotline.

Note: For more on the fall season, see **Autumnal Equinox**.

FLASH FLOOD

A flash flood means a dangerous rise in water levels in streams or over land in just a few hours. It's caused by heavy rain, ice jam break-up, an earthquake, or dam failure. Flash flooding is most common during the summer months. Some areas along the Scioto River, like Prospect and LaRue in Marion County, or Circleville in Pickaway County, or Piketon in Pike County, are prone to flash flooding.

FLASH FLOOD WARNING

A warning means flash flooding is either occurring or imminent along streams or other designated areas. Water levels will rise quickly, with the potential to wash away cars, buildings, and people. If you are in the warning area, you should take immediate precautions.

FLASH FLOOD WATCH

A watch means that flash flooding may soon occur in certain areas as the result of heavy rains or expected heavy rain. As with all watches, conditions are right for flash flooding to occur, but there are no guarantees.

FLOODING

Flooding is a natural and inevitable part of life along our country's streams and rivers. Flooding can be seasonal, a result of snow melt or of heavy rain. If the rain comes suddenly, it's called flash flooding. No part of our country is completely immune to flooding. In fact, flooding is the number one weather related killer nationally. Flash flooding can set water moving at tremendous speeds, moving rocks, ripping out trees, damaging buildings and homes, causing extensive property damage, even loss of life.

Flooding begins when the ground and plants can't absorb falling rain or melting snow and the runoff is so great that it can't be contained by the normal waterways or reservoirs. When water levels approach or exceed flood stage, the National Weather Service will issue regular flood statements, flood watches, and warnings. Fortunately, many flood warnings can be issued hours, or even days, in advance of the actual flooding. River flood warnings can sometimes be issued days or weeks in advance.

Eric Albrecht/The Columbus Dispatch

Flooding in New Richmond, Ohio, March 1997.

In central and southern Ohio, the Scioto, Sandusky, Hocking, and Ohio Rivers are all among those that are prone to flooding from time to time. In Ohio, winter and spring are the seasons with the best chance of significant flooding. Even though water levels don't rise as quickly as they tend to during the summer, they usually last longer and affect a larger area. Historic floods hit Ohio in 1913 and again in 1959. In 1959, all major streams in the state reached or exceeded flood stage from January 21–24.

As with all extreme weather conditions, flooding can be very dangerous. Here are some of the basic safety rules:

1. Do not attempt to cross rushing water on foot. The force of running water is surprisingly strong.

2. Do not drive through flooded areas. Abandon your vehicle if stuck in rising water and look for higher ground.

3. Be especially cautious at night when it's harder to see the danger.

Flood Safety Rules

FLOOD WATCH & WARNING

A flood watch is issued when heavy rain or snow melt is expected to cause water levels to rise over large portions of land. Typically, a watch is issued up to 18 hours ahead of potential flooding. A flood warning will be issued when flooding in a county or specific area will be confined to urban areas and/or small streams.

FOG

We all have those days when we feel like we're stuck in a fog. But in weather terminology, fog is basically a cloud on the ground. But not all fog is created equal. There are many kinds of fog. A few examples are listed below.

Steam Fog: This type of fog is common in fall and winter, especially around lakes, rivers, and streams. It's caused by cold air moving over warm water. It begins just a few inches over the water, where the air has cooled enough to cause condensation. And it kind of looks like wispy fingers reaching into the air above the water. Sometimes, though, it thickens into a localized pea soup kind of fog.

Ground Fog: Also called radiation fog, this is a shallow layer of fog created by the way the Earth "radiates" heat back into the environment on cool, clear nights with very light winds. The air near the ground cools below the dew point and condenses into fog. For this to happen, you need humid air near the ground and more humid air aloft. If there's too much wind, the drier air above will mix in and prevent the fog from forming. Ground fog is especially common in fall and winter, as well as in valley areas (valley fog).

Advection Fog: Advection refers to moving air. This type of fog is formed when moist air moves over a cool surface. This is especially common when warm air moves across snow covered ground. Again, the humid air is cooled below the dew point and fog forms.

Warm Front Fog: Fog can form when warm rain falls through the colder air ahead of a warm front. The rain evaporates into the cold air. The moisture is then cooled to the point where… you guessed it… fog forms. I sure hope this clears things up!

Steam Fog

FORECASTING

Bottom line, "fore"casting means predicting something be"fore" it actually happens. (That's the tricky part!) Unfortunately, there's no guarantee unless you're talking about something that has already happened. (Hindsight is 20/20.)

Today's forecasts are better than ever before, courtesy of faster, smarter computers and more data coming in from the field. The more data, the better the chances of an accurate forecast.

Much of the forecasting we do is based on a grid. Our forecasting models detect weather systems that pass over grid lines. Let me give you an example. Draw a tic-tac-toe board (see below).

Now, draw a couple of large circles big enough to intersect or overlap the lines (A, B, C). Those represent things (rain, snow, storms) that are big enough to be seen in the model; in other words, things that cross the grid lines show up in our forecast. But, if you make your circles small enough to fall inside the grid lines (D, E), the model won't see them, and they don't show up in the forecast. The only way to significantly improve forecasting is to increase the number of grid lines and reduce the amount of space between them.

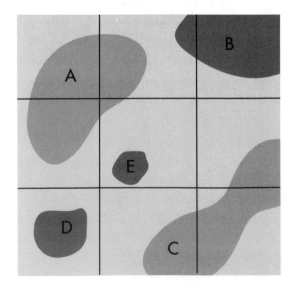

Note: You never hear politicians campaigning for more money to improve weathercasting. After all, that's VERY expensive. In fact, the government, to a large extent, is still the only entity that can afford to put satellites in space and Doppler Radars around the country. Private company forecasting has really grown in recent years, but the big models that come from the big computers still come from big government. (see **National Centers For Environmental Prediction** and **NOAA**)

As I mentioned in the introduction, TV stations do copious amounts of research to determine exactly what it is you want. Well, research says you, the public, demand a 5-day forecast. I'll give you three guesses which part of my whole presentation is probably the least accurate... and your first two guesses don't count. BINGO!

If there's any kind of error, even a small one, in the model we're using, it gets magnified all out of whack by the end of that 5-day period. Oddly enough, most viewers seem to instinctively know that going in, while others make set-in-stone decisions based on longer range outlooks. (Even I don't do that, and I made the forecast!)

Short term forecasts, say 12-24 hours, are pretty good these days. I'd say they're upwards of 80-90% accurate. But the further you go out, your accuracy, on average, really starts to drop. After about 4-5 days, you're really getting close to 50/50, meaning you're taking a guess. (Hopefully, an educated one.)

Of course, there are good seasons and bad seasons for forecasting. Personally, I find the transitional periods of spring and fall tougher in the temperature department. It's amazing how much difference a little cloud cover (or lack thereof) can really mess up your forecasted high or low.

FREEZE (FIRST & LAST)

In the fall, the cold weather seems to come way too early. In the spring, the cold seems to hang in there forever. But the first and last freezes of the year are among the first signs that the change of seasons is upon us.

Freezing, by the way, describes the change in a substance from liquid to solid. As a rule, freezing occurs around some kind of nucleus in the air or water, such as dust, salt, pollutants, dirt, or small clay particles. And here's a shocker. According to the Ohio Insurance Institute, frozen and broken water pipes rank second behind hurricanes in terms of the number of homes damaged and claim costs. So when that bitter cold comes, as it always seems to, here are a couple of tips for you.

Freeze Tips!

1. Add insulation wraps to water pipes, especially along outside walls.

2. Never set the thermostat below 55°F, even when gone for long periods.

3. Disconnect all outdoor hoses.

4. Consider draining water pipes before a long trip.

5. For bitter cold nights, leave the faucet on slow drip to keep water moving.

First and Last Freezes Throughout Central Ohio

	Average First Fall Freeze (32°F)	Average Last Spring Freeze (32°F)
Athens	October 1	May 16
Bellefontaine	October 11	May 3
Bucyrus	October 8	May 5
Chillicothe	October 15	April 22
Circleville	October 11	April 30
Columbus	October 17	April 16
Coshocton	October 8	May 6
Delaware/Lancaster	October 6	May 3
Gallipolis	October 10	April 30
Ironton	October 23	April 21
Kenton	October 7	May 4
London	October 7	May 2
Mansfield	October 17	May 9
Marietta	October 14	April 27
Marion	October 9	April 29
Marysville	October 9	May 2
Newark	October 8	May 3
New Lexington	October 4	May 7
Portsmouth	October 24	April 14
Washington C.H.	October 19	April 26
Xenia	October 13	April 29
Zanesville	October 6	May 6

source: National Weather Service

FREEZING RAIN

Freezing rain is an insidious thing. I've always thought that, of all winter weather conditions, this one's the worst. It's deceptive and dangerous because it develops quickly and without visible warning. Most of the time, you don't realize how slippery it is until you've stepped onto it or felt your car tires slipping. By then, it's usually too late.

Freezing rain starts as rain in air with temperatures above freezing. But once it hits a frozen surface, it freezes into a dangerous icy glaze. Even small accumulations of ice due to freezing rain can create serious hazards for drivers and pedestrians alike. What's more, this icy glaze covers tree branches and power lines. As a result, branches and power lines can become heavy and fall. Power outages are quite common during freezing rain and ice storms. Freezing rain drops are actually below 32°F, but have not yet turned into ice as they fall. Central Ohio averages between 10 and 14 days with freezing rain each year. West central and northwest Ohio see it somewhat more often, averaging 15–19 days each year.

FRONT

You can see fronts on every TV weather forecast. (But, for some reason, you almost never see backs.) We talk about them (fronts) all the time. And why not? When fronts come through, the weather changes. Quite simply, a front is a transition zone between two different air masses with different properties. There are four basic fronts you're likely to see on the TV (or any other) weather map. They are listed on the next page.

FYI: These staples of today's TV weather maps evolved during World War I. Norwegian meteorologists diligently built up a dense network of weather stations which gave a much better understanding of the principles of "frontal" weather. As a result, some days in TV it's a full frontal assault!

Cold Front

This is where cooler air advances, replacing warm air. It's a blue line with triangular barbs pointing in the direction the front is moving. Cold fronts tend to lift air dramatically, and may produce strong storms.

Warm Front

This is where warm air advances, replacing cooler air. It's a red line with semi-circles indicating the way it's moving. Warm fronts slope more gradually and may produce steady rain or snow over a longer period of time.

Stationary Front

As a forecaster, I hate these. This is where warmer air meets cooler air... but neither seems to be advancing. It's our job to determine (guess) when they'll start moving and where. These are drawn as alternating red and blue segments where the warm front and cold front barbs are pointing in opposite directions. Low pressure can slide along stationary fronts producing annoyingly repetitive conditions.

Occluded Front

Cold fronts move faster than warm fronts. And this is where the cold air overruns the warm air, lifting it upward. On the weather map it's a purple line with warm and cold front barbs pointing in the same direction. Occluded fronts often produce strong or severe storms along with strong gusty winds.

FROST

How many times do you wake up in the spring or fall only to find that, instead of the usual morning dew, there's a thin layer of sparkling white frost covering your front lawn? It's kind of a reminder that winter isn't very far behind/ahead. You're particularly surprised because your friendly neighborhood meteorologist said it would only get down to 36°F overnight. How can that be? Can I be right even with frost on the ground? Absolutely! Here's why.

"Official" low temperatures come from National Weather Service offices. Well, for readings that give a true picture of the air temperature, thermometers are kept in shielded enclosures about five feet off the ground. Meanwhile, temperatures at the ground can actually be colder due to the way the Earth radiates heat overnight. As a result, it can be 32°F at ground level, even though the overnight low will be reported at 36°F. Follow me? It seems like a contradiction, but it's not. And that's why I'll call for areas of frost even when I'm forecasting a morning low above freezing.

The temperature at which frost forms is called the frost point, making this the cold weather version of the dew point. Frost is made up of tiny ice crystals which form on grass and other surfaces when water vapor in the atmosphere freezes. This process is called sublimation.

FUJITA SCALE

If you've ever seen the movie *Twister*, or watched the evening news, for that matter, you've heard terms like "it was an F5, bandied about." For more context, it was an F5 that leveled Xenia back in 1974. The more recent Xenia tornado of 2000 was an F4. Both were particularly violent storms. But what do these terms mean?

Well, in weather we love to qualify, quantify, categorize, and catalogue. In this case, we owe the terminology to a dedicated scientist and researcher named Tetsuya Theodore (Ted) Fujita (1920 – 1998).

Back in the 1970s, Fujita developed the rating system we still use today. It's called the Fujita Scale of Tornado Intensity, and it's a way of directly relating damage to wind speed. The Fujita Scale refers to the level of damage, rather than the actual tornado.

The vast majority of tornadoes, nearly 3/4, are classified as weak on the Fujita Scale (F0 to F1). By contrast, just one percent of all tornados can be classified as violent, F4 – F5, but these account for nearly 2/3 of all tornado related deaths.

Ted Fujita's analysis of the Super Outbreak of 1974, which included the massive Xenia tornado as well as 147 others, was particularly enlightening. Fujita was able to plot most of the tornadoes using Fujita Scale contours, showing the ebb and flow of the storms.

Through the same analysis, he also identified new types of wind damage, which you now routinely hear us talk about on TV, the downburst and the microburst.

Fujita Scale

Fujita Tornado Intensity Scale

FO–F1	F2–F3	F4–F5
weak	strong	violent

Developed in 1971 by T. Theodore Fujita of the University of Chicago

F0	40–72 mph	Gale Tornado—light damage. Some damage to chimneys; break branches off trees; push over shallow-rooted trees; damage sign boards.
F1	73–112 mph	Moderate Tornado—moderate damage. The lower limit is the beginning of hurricane wind speed; peel surface off roofs; mobile homes pushed off foundations or overturned; moving autos pushed off the roads.
F2	113–157 mph	Significant Tornado—considerable damage. Roofs torn off frame houses; mobile homes demolished; boxcars pushed over; large trees snapped or uprooted; light-objects missiles generated.
F3	158–206 mph	Severe Tornado—severe damage. Roofs and some walls torn off well-constructed houses; trains overturned; most trees in forest uprooted; heavy cars lifted off the ground and thrown.
F4	207–260 mph	Devastating Tornado—devastating damage. Well-constructed houses leveled; structures with weak foundations blown off some distance; cars thrown and large missiles generated.
F5	261–318 mph	Incredible Tornado—incredible damage. Strong frame houses lifted off foundations and carried considerable distance to disintegrate; automobile-sized missiles fly through the air in excess of 100 meters (109 yds);
F6-F12	319 mph –MACH 1 (speed of sound)	The maximum winds speeds of tornadoes are not expected to reach the F6 wind speeds.

GEOGRAPHY

Where you live plays a huge role in what kind of weather you have. Geography is one of the biggest reasons for this. Say you live by the ocean or one of the Great Lakes. Water temperatures change much more slowly than air temperatures. That's why you'd have to be a member of the polar bear club to go swimming during much of the spring because, even though the air temperature has warmed up, the water is still pretty cold. Then again, the water tends to stay warm for a while, even when summer's heat has started to fade. That explains why the lakeshore area of Ohio stays a little warmer overnight in the late fall and early winter than much of inland Ohio. The trade-off is that Lake Erie also provides the moisture for lake-effect snow during the winter months in the infamous snow belt of Ohio. (You take the good with the bad.)

Similarly, mountains can affect the movement of storms. (And air in general. Though, admittedly, mountains aren't a big weather-maker in Ohio.) Wind hitting the side of a mountain can be deflected upward. Of course, as air rises, it cools and clouds may form. On the windward side of the mountain, heavy rain can result from this uplift. This is seen in the area west of the Rockies. The opposite thing can happen on the "lee" side of the mountains, where there is often a rain shadow.

Not all geographic features occur naturally either. Scientists now believe that large urban areas can have an impact on localized weather. (see **Urban Heat Island**)

GLOBAL WARMING

Here's one of those hot topics you can expect to be hotly debated over the next few years as more and more studies come out. Most of us probably have an opinion on the subject. But how do you separate fact from fiction?

The theory of global warming speculates that the Earth's atmosphere is slowly warming due to the increasing amount of man-made gases that absorb and give off heat. These gases include chlorofluorocarbons (CFCs), carbon dioxide, and methane. As is the case in so many things, scientists continue to debate the extent of the threat.

Scientists at The Ohio State University's Byrd Polar Research Center are studying huge ice cores from China in an effort to learn what our atmosphere used to be like, so that they can compare it to the present. Some of these studies seem to confirm that man's production of carbon dioxide really is threatening to overheat our world, eventually melting the ice caps and causing the oceans to rise.

The skeptics, however, argue that recent global warming trends are merely a natural variation in the climate, much as we see the occasionally cold or overly warm winter. Ironically, as we talk about global warming, recent volcanic eruptions have shot enough dust into the atmosphere so as to offset the process, temporarily. Meanwhile, it also appears that ozone destruction, due to CFCs, may serve to counterbalance some of the warming.

In any case, the debate and the battle rages on.

GOOD FORECAST

Wow! Talk about debatable. Exactly what is a "good" forecast? Let me tell you a little story. The station got a call from a kid who had just finished a science fair project. He wanted me to know that after a month of comparing the forecasts on all three stations and in the newspaper, mine was right the most. GREAT, we thought.

Seizing on the promotional opportunity, we went live from the science fair that night. When I got there, I had very little time to spare, and no opportunity to "pre-interview" the student. When I asked him about the results, his response was, "you were right most often... and you were only right once!"

Of course, I turned three shades of red, and stammered something to the effect of, "what do you mean?" His response to me was that if the forecast called for a low of 32 and a high of 50, if the actual high and low were 49 and 31, the forecast was wrong. Ouch! I would have considered that a VERY good forecast.

Truth be told, the only readings that "count" in Columbus are the readings at the airport. (Have you ever met anyone who actually lives at the airport?) Observations are also taken at several other locations in and around the metro area. Guess what. Not only do the temperatures vary from Point A to Point B, but so does the barometric pressure, the relative humidity, the wind, even rain and snow.

No question, the best forecast would be a perfect one. But basically, what we're doing is trying to predict the conditions at the airport... where no one lives. For my money, a "good" forecast is one that's "in the ballpark" when it comes to temperature, sky conditions, and precipitation. The debate is over how big is the ballpark. Wouldn't life be easier in a domed stadium?

GREENHOUSE EFFECT

It's the same principle behind why a greenhouse stays warm in the winter, and the inside of your car heats up enough to bake a pizza in the summer. (A word of warning: be careful on those aforementioned hot, summer days if you're wearing shorts and have dark vinyl or leather upholstery.)

Unlike a greenhouse, the Earth isn't surrounded by glass (at least, I don't think so), but it is wrapped in its atmosphere. Temperatures warm at and near the surface because of the absorption and "re-emission" of infrared radiation by the water vapor and carbon dioxide that are present in the atmosphere. This type of warming would not be possible without the thin layer of atmosphere near the surface. Our atmosphere also helps contain the heat, much the way your car's interior or a greenhouse heats up and stays warm for a long period of time afterward. The greenhouse effect, since it's affected by carbon dioxide, goes hand in hand with the problem of global warming.

GROUNDHOG DAY

It sneaks up on me every year. I have to admit that some years I can relate to Bill Murray's movie about the TV weatherman who's stuck reliving that one day over and over again. The truth be told, they do not teach us about this in meteorology school. Even so, they might as well, since it comes up every year on February 2nd.

I guess the blame should be put on old Punxatawney Phil, that furry Pennsylvania pest who, by now, must be quite ancient. Anyway, with more than a little help, the chubby little creature supposedly emerges from his burrow each year on this date to look for his shadow. If he sees it, legend goes, it means to expect six more weeks of winter. (Apparently the shadow scares him, and he runs back into his hole.) If he doesn't see his shadow, it means to expect an early spring. I guess we should pray for gray days. (A good bet during Ohio's long winter.)

If Phil seems too far away, you only have to look to "Buckeye Chuck," possibly a relative of Phil's from Marion, Ohio.

GROWING SEASON

The length of the growing season varies dramatically from place to place across this great country of ours. The length of the season is determined by the amount of days between the first and last freezes of the season (see **Freeze**). In warmer cities like Los Angeles or Miami, entire years may pass without a freeze. Of course, we couldn't be that lucky here in the Buckeye state. (After all, isn't it the change of seasons that draws people here in the first place?)

Here's a shocker. The average growing season in Duluth, Minnesota is just 125 days. It's just three days longer than that in Lander, Wyoming. Think about it. That's only four months! You can squeak out an extra week, on average, if you were to move to Bismarck, North Dakota. In Columbus, by comparison, it's almost tropical. We can sneak out close to six months, with just slight variations to the north and south.

GULF COAST LOW

These little babies can be nasty in the winter, giving central Ohio some of its heaviest snowfalls on record. (The Blizzard of 1978 was one such storm.) These intense areas of low pressure (see **L**) tend to form down in the Louisiana Delta and migrate northward toward Ohio dragging copious amounts of Gulf Coast moisture along with them.

Depending on the track these storms take, we can get either heavy rain or heavy snow... and sometimes both.

During the winter, if the center of the low remains east of the state, we get the moisture from the backside of the low. Combined with the typical cold of the season, that can mean a very wet snow, the kind kids love for making snowmen and snowballs.

If, however, the storm center migrates west of the state, the milder Gulf air on the eastern side of the low may change any snow into rain. (Put the sleds back in the garage and dig out your umbrellas.)

H

What the heck is that big blue "H" on the weather map? I often ask school kids that question. Their answers vary. I've heard: "high temperatures," "hot," "humid," "hazy," and "huh?" But I often hear "high pressure." Ding, Ding, Ding! Good Answer. High pressure it is. As a rule, you can also think of the big "H" as "happy weather." After all, high pressure often gives us sunshine and dry days. Of course, there are exceptions to every rule. (That's especially true in the weather "biz.")

The technical name for high pressure in the atmosphere is anticyclone, which means that the air flow around the high is clockwise. If you're east of an approaching high, you'll get cool northerly winds. On the backside,

> **Trivia:** Air under high pressure warms as it falls. This is called compression. The same principle explains why a bike pump heats up as you fill up your tires. The air warms as it is compressed.

you'll feel winds coming out of the south, which typically means hot and sticky in the summertime. At least, that's the way it works north of the equator. Everything flows the opposite direction in the Southern Hemisphere. (Including the water you let out of the tub or flush down the toilet. Again, it's a case of perspective due to the forces created by the spinning of the Earth on its axis.)

The air beneath high pressure is usually falling, warming as it falls. This subsiding motion can suppress the development of clouds. It can also lead to inversions which can bottle up pollution and create stagnant, unhealthy air. But, as a rule, advancing high pressure is usually a sign that nice, dry weather is coming.

Folklore: Gaining weight? It's been said that you'll put on a pound or two as high pressure moves in behind a cold front.

HAIL

Hailstones are a sign of an especially intense thunderstorm. The bigger the hail, the bigger the storm! Hail forms in the strong updrafts of towering cumulonimbus (thunderstorm) clouds. If you were to cut open a hailstone, what you would see are concentric rings of clear and opaque ice. The rings tell the story of each hailstone's history, much like the rings in the trunk of a tree.

Hailstones are born in the upper part of a strong thunderstorm where moisture can actually exist at below freezing temperatures. The size of the hailstone depends on the strength of the updrafts and the number of trips up and down within these towering storms. The layers of clear ice form when the hailstone falls through very moist air, so that water accumulates faster than it can freeze. The darker, opaque layers form when the stones fall through air with smaller and fewer cloud droplets, which freeze instantly on impact, trapping air bubbles in the process.

Hail is particularly damaging to farm crops. An entire season's crop may be lost during a hail storm. Hailstones can range in size from tiny, ice pellets, to baseball and even softball size! Funny thing is, while hail and thunderstorms go hand in hand, the region of the United States with the most thunderstorms every year, Florida, has one of the lowest hail rates. In fact, Florida averages less than one hail storm per season at any given place. The hail capital of the U.S. is actually southeastern Wyoming, which averages up to eight or nine hail producing thunderstorms per season at any one place.

NOAA/National Severe Storms Laboratory

Note: Hailstones are usually spherical. But there are verified reports of flat hailstones, saucer-shaped stones, even some covered with sharp spikes.

HALO

Halos are one of those phenomena that always prompt calls to the 10TV Weather Center. "What is it? What does it mean?" Well, a halo is a bright ring that appears around the Moon or the Sun. Halos are generally white with a faint reddish tint on the inside of the ring and a smidgen of violet on the outside. Halos are a sign that there are ice crystals in the air, and you're looking at the Moon (or the Sun) through these ice crystals. Typically, this means that there are cirrus-type clouds, found high in the sky, which foreshadow approaching warm-front rain.

By the way, the angle between the Sun and the halo is 22 degrees, because of the way light is refracted through the six-sided ice crystals. (See, every part of nature's beauty can be reduced to a far less poetic equation!) By the way, winter fog can produce a similar effect.

Folklore: "Ring around the Moon, rain or snow coming soon."

HEAT INDEX

In an area where the "normal" high never hits 90°F, we always seem to get more than our fair share of steamy, summer days. In fact, the words hazy, hot, and humid often dominate my late-summer forecast. But it's that humid part that seems to bother us the most. When we say "it feels more like a hundred," we're usually complaining about the relative humidity.

In the desert southwest, the normal high easily, and often, exceeds 100°F for weeks at a time. They say, "Yes, but it's dry heat." So what is it about the heat in Ohio? One of the terms we forecasters use is "heat index." And I, for one, get lots of questions about what the heat index is. My standard answer is, "It's how warm and uncomfortable it feels because of the combination of heat and humidity." In other words, the thermometer reads 94°F, but if the relative humidity is sixty percent, then it feels more like 112°F.

When the heat index is high, drink plenty of fluids and avoid over exertion. But that's only the *Reader's Digest* version of the heat index. Some folks are more persistent. "What's the formula so I can figure it out myself?" I warn them not to go to all the trouble. I have a handy-dandy little graph that will do that for you. All you need are the temperature and relative humidity. But some still persist. So, for all of you who want to take what we try to make simple and make it complicated again, here goes.

If you want to get really technical, here's the actual heat index equation:

$$\begin{aligned}
\text{H.I.} = \ & -42.379 + 2.04901523T + \\
& 10.14333127R - 0.22475541TR \\
& - 6.83783 \times 10^{-3}T^2 - 5.481717 \times \\
& 10^{-2}R^2 + 1.22874 \times 10^{-3}T^2R \times \\
& 8.5282 \times 10^{-4}TR^2 - 1.99 \times \\
& 10^{-6}T^2R^2 .
\end{aligned}$$

R = Relative Humidity
T = Temperature in Degrees Fahrenheit

(Personally, I prefer the little chart on the next page.)

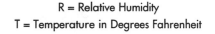

The heat index is a combination of the following: vapor pressure, the surface area of the human skin, effective radiation of the skin, the body's volume and density, clothing cover, core density and vapor pressure, surface temperatures and vapor pressures of skin and clothing, activity level, effective wind speed, clothing resistance to heat and moisture transfer, radiation and convection from the skin's surface, sweating rate, ventilation rate, skin resistance to heat and moisture transfer and surface resistance to heat and moisture transfer. (What a mouthful! I warned you.)

Heat Index

Heat Index	Affects on the human body
130° or above	heat stroke likely with contined exposure
105° to 130°	heat stroke likely with prolonged exposure
90° to 105°	heat stroke possible with prolonged exposure

		Actual Air Temperature (°F)								
		75	80	85	90	95	100	105	110	115
		Apparent Temperature								
Relative Humidity	30	73	78	84	90	96	104	113	123	135
	35	73	79	85	91	98	107	118	130	143
	40	74	79	86	93	101	110	123	137	151
	45	74	80	87	95	104	115	129	143	
	50	75	81	88	96	107	120	135	150	
	55	75	81	89	98	110	126	142		
	60	76	82	90	100	114	132	149		
	65	76	83	91	102	119	138			
	70	77	85	93	106	124	144			
	75	77	86	95	109	130				
	80	78	86	97	113	136				
	85	78	87	99	117					
	90	79	88	102	122					
	95	79	89	105						
	100	80	91	108						

source: National Weather Service

HEAT WAVE

A heat wave is a period of uncomfortable, or even dangerous, heat that can last days or weeks. If they last long enough, heat waves can kill. That's exactly what happened in Chicago during the summer of 1995. Here are some basic safety rules to follow during a heat wave or anytime the heat and humidity get too high.

1. Slow down. Avoid strenuous activities or wait until nighttime when it's cooler.

2. Stay out of the sun.

3. Spend time in air-conditioned areas. If this isn't possible, stay on the lowest floor where it tends to stay cooler. Get a fan. Although fans do not cool the air, they will cool your skin through evaporation of sweat.

4. Wear light-weight and light-colored clothing. Avoid heat-absorbing black or navy.

5. Drink lots of water. Avoid alcohol and caffeine.

6. Check on the elderly.

7. Don't forget your pet. Give pets plenty of fresh water and shade.

8. Don't leave kids or pets in you car. Remember that Greenhouse Effect. (CDs and videotapes will melt too, although they can usually be replaced.)

Tips!

HURRICANE

Hurricanes are something else! They're the "greatest storm on earth!" Just ask my 10TV co-anchor, Angela Pace. She was on the Island of St. Thomas when Hurricane Marilyn ripped it apart during September of 1995. Wind gusts were measured at 175 miles per hour! "The wind roared like lions," Angela told me, as corrugated steel roofs were ripped off the buildings there. Many of the buildings went with them.

OK. That said, let's set the record straight. We don't have hurricanes in Ohio. Hurricanes are creatures of the water. They fade fast over land. And with the exception of Lake Erie, we're pretty well land-locked here. Of course, we don't have hurricanes over Lake Erie either. We're talking warm, tropical ocean water. That's where a hurricane's energy comes from.

Hurricanes are the biggest storms on Earth. Their winds can extend out for hundreds of miles. Hurricanes are huge whirlwinds that develop in the tropics as loosely organized showers and thunderstorms. As this tropical storm becomes more organized and starts moving westward, it grows and intensifies through several distinct stages.

Hurricane Stages

1. **Easterly Wave:** a wave or trough of low pressure moving east to west.

2. **Tropical Disturbance:** a low pressure region of clouds & showers in the trade winds region.

3. **Tropical Depression:** a more organized area of low pressure with winds blowing counter-clockwise. Winds: up to 31 mph.

4. **Tropical Storm:** This is where they first get a name. Winds now: 32–73 mph.

5. **Hurricane:** The big one! Winds: 74 mph & higher.

Saffir-Simpson Hurricane Scale:

Category 1:	74–95 mph	Minimal
Category 2:	96–110 mph	Moderate
Category 3:	111–130 mph	Extensive
Category 4:	131–155 mph	Extreme
Category 5:	155 mph +	Catastrophic

Once they reach maturity, hurricanes are made up of huge spiral bands of rain and thunderstorms. The deeper you get into the storm, the stronger the winds. Of course, like with all kinds of weather, to every rule there is an exception. That's especially true with hurricanes. Smack in the middle of a hurricane is an area of complete calm. The rain stops, the winds die down, and warm air is falling rather than rising. The Sun may even be shining! This area is called the "eye" of the storm. And it passes over just as the hurricane appears to reach its worst.

NOAA GOES photo processed by H. Michael Mogil

Hurricane Lane spins south of Baja California on September 10, 2000 in this GOES Infrared image. The eye and eye wall are well defined in this specially enhanced image.

From space, a hurricane with a well-developed eye looks like a big doughnut or bagel. But, startling as it can be, the eye is only a brief break from the incredible force of the storm. The area immediately surrounding the eye, called the eye wall, contains the strongest winds of all and can cause incredible amounts of damage.

Unlike tornadoes, which develop quickly, making them tough to predict, there's lots of warning as hurricanes develop. The tough part is predicting their path. As they move out of the tropical Atlantic, they usually move east to west. As they move further north, they usually turn more to the east or northeast. Unfortunately, they tend to wobble and move erratically, making it very difficult to predict exactly where the eye will come ashore. Hurricane watches and warnings, though, are issued for large areas well in advance of the storm's arrival.

Historically speaking, as far as Atlantic hurricanes go, the three stormiest years were 1933 — with 31 tropical storms (10 became hurricanes) — and then a tie between 1995 and 1969, each year had 30 tropical storms. (Twelve became hurricanes in 1969 and eleven in 1995.) Hurricane Opal, which hit the Florida panhandle in October 1995 and left 59 dead, became the third most costly storm to hit the United States since Andrew in 1992 and Hugo in 1989. By the way, the Atlantic hurricane season runs from May until November. September has traditionally been the month with the most (and worst) hurricanes.

Note: The name hurricane comes from the Spanish "huracán," which probably comes from the Mayan storm god "Hunraken" or "Hurakan" the Quiche god of thunder and lightning.

Fun Fact: One hour of hurricane energy is equal to all the electric power generated in the United States over an entire year.

HURRICANE NAMES

This was a big topic of discussion in 1995 as the Atlantic hurricane season made it deeper into the alphabet than it ever had since they began naming tropical storms in 1950. The names are chosen by the World Meteorological Organization (WMO). They are alphabetical and on a five-year cycle of alternating male and female names. Although, until 1978, all hurricane names were feminine.

The calls started coming in after Pablo, when we skipped "Q" and went directly to Roxanne. The WMO decided that there just aren't enough names beginning with Q, U, X, Y, and Z (although we had lots of suggestions). And although we only made it as far as Tanya, had we passed Van and Wendy, we would have moved on to the Greek Alphabet: Hurricane Alpha, Hurricane Beta, etc. Go figure. It's all Greek to me. The great English writer, William Shakespeare, never at a loss for words, might have said: "Alas, poor hurricane Yorrick..."

Speaking of names, hurricanes aren't even called "hurricanes" worldwide. They're called "typhoons" in the western Pacific and eastern Asia, "baguios" in the Philippines and China Sea, and "cyclones" in Australia, the Indian Ocean, and the Bay of Bengal.

FYI: The Atlantic hurricane names for 2001-2005 are listed on the next page.

2001	2002	2003	2004	2005
Allison	Arthur	Ana	Alex	Arlene
Barry	Bertha	Bill	Bonnie	Bret
Chantal	Cristobal	Claudette	Charley	Cindy
Dean	Dolly	Danny	Danielle	Dennis
Erin	Edouard	Erika	Earl	Emily
Felix	Fay	Fabian	Frances	Franklin
Gabrielle	Gustav	Grace	Gaston	Gert
Humberto	Hanna	Henri	Hermine	Harvey
Iris	Isidore	Isabel	Ivan	Irene
Jerry	Josephine	Juan	Joanne	Jose
Karen	Kyle	Kate	Karl	Katrina
Lorenzo	Lili	Larry	Lisa	Lee
Michelle	Marco	Mindy	Matthew	Maria
Noel	Nana	Nicholas	Nicole	Nate
Olga	Omar	Odette	Otto	Ophelia
Pablo	Paloma	Peter	Paula	Philippe
Rebekah	Rene	Rose	Richard	Rita
Sebastien	Sally	Sam	Shary	Stan
Tanya	Teddy	Teresa	Tomas	Tammy
Van	Vicky	Victor	Virginie	Vince
Wendy	Wilfred	Wanda	Walter	Wilma

ICE JAM

An Ice Jam is a popular cold-weather, outdoor concert, typically involving heavy metal bands. (Kidding… again.) Actually, ice jams can be VERY dangerous. When broken ice gets caught in a narrow channel, it can cause serious localized flooding. Ice jams are most common during late winter and early spring thaws. While this kind of flooding is weather related, in a general sense, it's tricky to forecast without specific local river information.

ICICLES

You might call them "winter's decorations." After all, in climates like ours, you can find them hanging around everywhere. They dangle from roofs, eaves, ledges, tree limbs, anywhere that water freezes due to snowmelt, rain, mist, spray, or seeping water. But even though we see them all the time, how many of us actually take the time to stop and take a real look at them?

If you did, you'd see that icicles are typically cone shaped and, in extreme cases, can grow to be several feet long. Upon closer examination, you might notice that newly formed icicles often have a ribbed appearance from the rings that form during the growth process. Horizontal ribs are a sign of steady growth, while vertical ribs are a sign of renewed growth after a period of dormancy. You'll also notice air bubbles trapped within the ice. If there are enough small bubbles, the icicle will take on a whitish appearance.

Icicles

Here's some icy trivia. If an icicle is growing, the tip of the icicle will be mostly liquid, with a pendant shaped water drop at the end. Icicles also grow downward and outward at the same time, but at different speeds. What's more, if you watch an icicle over a long period of time, you'll see that it changes over time. As ice gradually changes into water vapor, the surface smoothes out. And since icicles are made up of many tiny ice crystals, their internal appearance changes as they melt.

Kids Note: If you don't have easy access to naturally occurring icicles, you can make your own by dripping cold water off a solid object in freezing weather.

INDIAN SUMMER

This one sometimes seems like a generic term to describe any late-season warm spell. Actually, it's a period of abnormally warm weather in mid-to-late autumn with clear skies and cool nights. Many insist that a first frost must precede this warm spell. Regardless of the precise definition, it's one of the few things I receive almost no complaints about.

INVERSION

This is one of those cases where the normal rules just don't apply. Normally, temperature falls with height, typically by about three degrees per thousand feet. But in an inversion, there's a level of warm air above a layer of cooler air near the ground. This layer of warm air keeps the cooler air from rising, trapping it near the surface. If an inversion persists, the air can become stagnant, trapping pollution and fog for long periods of time. This is particularly common in cities located in valleys or surrounded by mountains. (Just ask the folks in LA or Denver… even Las Vegas.)

IRONTON

Located in the famous "hanging rock" iron district of southern Ohio, in Lawrence County, the city was at the center of southern Ohio's pig iron industry. The weather can be quite warm in the summer, and the winters are understandably milder than in central and northern Ohio.

FYI: The name, which seems as self-explanatory as any, is probably a contraction of iron and town, or Irontown.

Average Temperature (in degrees Fahrenheit) and Precipitation (in inches) for Ironton, Ohio

(Elevation: 555 feet)

Month	Temperature High	Low	Precipitation	Snowfall
January	41	21	2.55	7
February	46	24	2.78	5
March	58	33	3.06	3
April	67	42	3.50	0
May	78	51	3.98	0
June	85	60	3.57	0
July	88	64	4.58	0
August	87	63	3.77	0
September	81	56	2.59	0
October	70	44	2.80	0
November	58	35	2.93	1
December	46	27	3.13	3

source: National Weather Service

JET STREAM

Jet streams are like narrow rivers of strong wind in the upper atmosphere. They can have a big influence steering weather systems around the globe. In the United States, there are actually two jet streams to keep an eye on. The "polar jet" is the one that dives down from Canada in the winter bringing cold air and occasional storms across Ohio. The other is the "sub-tropical jet," which doesn't meander as much as the polar jet, but often steers warm tropical air across the southern half of the U.S.

Jet streams change position from day to day and throughout the year. We talk about them on the weather to explain why temperatures change so much and why storm systems move the way they do. Funny thing is, jet streams were only a theory until 1946. That's when high-flying military aircraft ran into strong head winds that made flying east to west extremely difficult. Even today, you'll notice that flying cross-country east to west usually takes longer than flying west to east. The reason: the nice west to east tail wind supplied by this meandering river of wind, fittingly called the jet stream.

For example, say you're on a 2000-mile eastbound flight. With a 150 miles per hour jet stream, the journey would take about three hours and four minutes. On the return flight, flying at the same altitude, the westbound journey would take four hours and forty-three minutes!

KERAUNOPHOBIA

Although you'd never know it from the name, keraunophobia is a fear of thunderstorms. (Oprah needs to do a show on this!) I've always gotten calls from parents with kids who are terrified by thunderstorms. Fear, of course, is unhealthy, so I always emphasize awareness and a healthy respect for the sometimes violent forces of nature. Teaching kids the safety rules about thunderstorms is critical. Hopefully by understanding and respecting the world around us, kids can alleviate their fears. (see **Thunder**)

KNOT

William Shakespeare once said, "To be or knot to be. That is the question." Knot! All kidding aside, this is an important weather term. A knot is a unit of speed. In weather, it's most often heard in a marine or lake forecast, but it also turns up on certain pressure charts. Knot is short for nautical miles per hour. A knot equals 1.152 miles per hour. The Lake Erie forecast always gives the wind speed in knots.

Easy rough conversion: For every 7 knots (kt) of wind speed in a lake forecast, add 1 mile per hour (mph) to convert to miles per hour. A 7 kt wind is about 8 mph; a 14 kt wind, 16 mph; and a 21 kt wind, 24 mph.

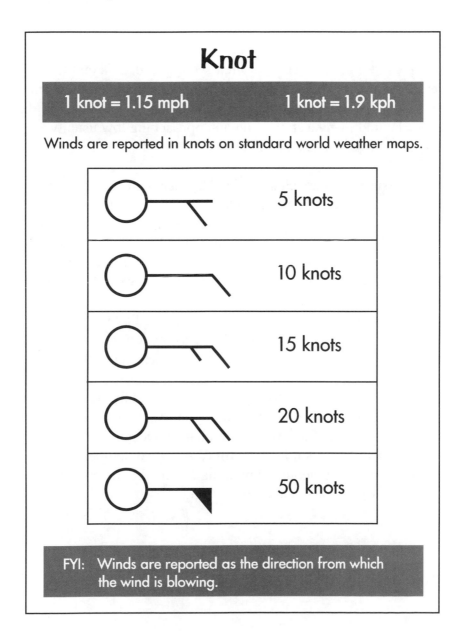

Knot

1 knot = 1.15 mph   1 knot = 1.9 kph

Winds are reported in knots on standard world weather maps.

	5 knots
	10 knots
	15 knots
	20 knots
	50 knots

FYI: Winds are reported as the direction from which the wind is blowing.

L

Just like the big, blue "H", we often see big, red "L"s on the weather map. The "L" stands for Low pressure. You often see the big "L" with some kind of front attached to it. Low pressure is the culprit behind many a storm, and an approaching low usually means bye-bye sunshine, hello clouds.

Low pressure areas are characterized by rising air which forms clouds. As such, I've heard that the "L" actually stands for lousy weather. In a way, that's often true. But technically speaking, a low is actually a cyclone (a term that is used to refer to tornadoes and still applies to hurricanes). Air around cyclones (low pressure) moves counterclockwise (see **Backside of the Low**). As a low pressure center approaches from the west, you'll experience a warmer, southerly flow of air, carried northward by the southerly winds. But (and there's always a "but") as the low moves east, the winds start coming out of the north on the backside of the low.

Since the big "L" and frontal systems are so closely connected, an approaching low typically means that you should expect the winds to pick up and the weather to change. Depending on the season, it's sometimes rain, sometimes snow, sometimes storms, and sometimes just clouds. Maybe that's why the meteorologist is sometimes right… and sometimes wrong.

LAKE-EFFECT SNOW

If you have any questions about the impact of geography on weather, just pay a visit to Ashtabula, Geauga, or Lake County in northeast Ohio some winter when a north wind comes blowing across Lake Erie.

The principle is pretty simple. Lake-effect snow showers are generated when cold, dry air moves across a warm lake surface. (The Great Lakes are especially known for this phenomenon.) These cold, typically northwesterly winds pick up both moisture and heat and can produce tremendous amounts of snow on the "lee" side of the lake. Lake effect snowfall is most common in northeast Ohio during the late fall and early winter months.

LAKE ERIE

You might call this Great Lake the "Great Weather-Maker," for all the impact it has on Ohio. Why do you think Ohio has a snow belt? During winter, cold northerly winds pick up moisture from the lake and dump it as snow all over northeast Ohio. But beyond the snow belt, even central Ohio receives lake-effect snow from time to time. And we CERTAINLY get lake effect clouds over the winter.

Then again, for communities bordering the lake, the water can actually help regulate the temperature. You see, water temperatures change much more slowly than air temperatures. As a result, warmer lake waters can help keep coastal areas milder during the fall and early winter, while the cooler waters can help cool the coastline during spring and early summer.

Boaters beware! Waterspouts occur at certain times of the year, especially when cool air passes over warm lake waters. And while a popular recreation area for boating, fishing, and tourism, conditions on the water can change very rapidly. Boaters need to be on the lookout for marine warnings like small craft advisories and gale warnings.

LA NIÑA

Meet El Niño's little sister. La Niña winters tend to be far more brutal, cold, and snowy than her big brother's. While El Niño brings warmer than normal ocean currents to the west coasts of North and South America, La Niña brings atypically cool waters that can also have a major impact on weather across the country. Ohio typically gets more snow, longer cold snaps, and there's no hurricane suppressing side effects in the Atlantic. The winter of 1995-1996 was a good example of a La Niña winter. Columbus got a near record snowfall of 54.1 inches. It even snowed in April! That same year, Cleveland was buried under a record 101 inches.

LIGHTNING

Lightning strikes the Earth about three billion times each year... and there's a lot more of it up in the clouds that never makes it down here. Lightning is a spectacular illustration of nature's balancing act. It's caused by the build up of huge static electric charges within clouds or between a cloud and the ground. It is, at once, one of nature's most dramatic and deadly phenomena. Friction created by rising air tends to build strong positive charges in the tops of thunderheads, while a basically negative charge builds in the lower part of the cloud. Similarly, the Earth usually has a negative charge.

Lightning is Mother Nature's way of releasing these stored up charges. The lightning bolt, in a blinding flash, connects the opposite charges, generating tremendous amounts of heat (to the tune of about 50,000 degrees)! This causes the air to expand very quickly, then slam back together producing a shock wave we hear as thunder (see **Thunder**). Lightning typically occurs within a cloud, goes cloud to ground or cloud to cloud, as strong opposite charges build up within active storms. Because it moves so fast (at the speed of light), it's often tough to determine a starting and ending point. Researchers have even discovered a rare type of lightning that shoots from the top of a thunderstorm, straight up toward space!

By the way, it was Benjamin Franklin's famous kite experiment in 1752 that proved that lightning is a powerful discharge of electricity. But kids, do not try this at home! In other words, no kite-flying during a thunderstorm. Other things you should avoid during a storm — since all thunderstorms contain lightning — are

standing alone in an open field, talking on the phone, and taking a shower, since metal pipes and phone wires can both conduct electricity. Also, July is typically the deadliest month. For one thing, there are lots of thunderstorms. But it's also a popular time of year for outdoor activities.

Keep in mind, while typically thought of as a summer phenomenon, lightning does occur during winter snow storms and blizzards. In fact, when it does occur, it seems especially strong and loud. Winter storms with enough energy to generate lightning can produce snowfalls of around three inches per hour.

Safety Tip: Tall trees offer no protection against lightning strikes. In fact, they can serve as lightning rods and actually attract lightning. What's more, even if you're not immediately under a tree, the roots will conduct electricity too. So steer clear of tall trees during a storm. What about your car? Will it protect you? You bet! And there are four very good reasons why. Your tires. The rubber wheels ground your car, making it a safe haven during a thunderstorm. But what if you're caught out in the open? The best thing you can do, should you feel your hair standing on end, is lie flat on the ground.

Folklore: "Beware the oak, it draws the stroke. Avoid the ash, it draws the flash. But beneath the thorn, you'll come to no harm."

FYI: According to NASA, the Earth is struck by lightning every three seconds.

MANSFIELD

Nestled in the central highlands of Ohio, Mansfield has a somewhat different climate than Ohio's three biggest cities. After all, the elevation is considerably higher above sea level. This fact, combined with its close proximity to the snow track in northern Ohio makes it a snowier place than Columbus. Mansfield is the county seat of Richland County. It's also one of Ohio's winter destinations as a ski area. (That's where that snow really comes in handy.)

FYI: The city was named after the Surveyor General of the United States, Colonel Jared Mansfield, under whose instructions the city was laid out.

MARIETTA

This historic southeast Ohio city in Washington County is located at the mouth of the Muskingum River and is also nestled along the mighty Ohio River. At less than half the elevation, Marietta is a world apart from Mansfield (above). It warms up more quickly and gets far less snow.

FYI: The city was named Marietta in honor of Marie Antoinette of France.

Average Temperature (in degrees Fahrenheit) and Precipitation (in inches) for Mansfield, Ohio

(Elevation: 1295 feet)

Month	Temperature High	Low	Precipitation	Snowfall
January	32	17	1.65	10
February	35	19	1.66	9
March	47	29	2.88	7
April	59	38	3.43	2
May	69	48	4.15	0
June	78	57	3.68	0
July	82	62	3.67	Are you kidding?
August	80	60	4.00	0
September	78	57	2.88	0
October	62	43	2.08	Trace
November	49	34	3.12	2
December	37	23	2.82	9

source: National Weather Service

Average Temperature (in degrees Fahrenheit) and Precipitation (in inches) for Marietta, Ohio

(Elevation: 580 feet)

Month	Temperature High	Low	Precipitation	Snowfall
January	39	21	2.36	8
February	43	22	2.49	5
March	54	32	3.11	Trace
April	65	40	2.84	0
May	75	50	3.62	0
June	83	59	3.64	0
July	86	63	3.90	Not a Chance.
August	84	62	3.33	0
September	78	55	3.01	0
October	67	43	2.69	0
November	55	35	2.77	2
December	44	26	2.91	4

source: National Weather Service

MARINE WEATHER

Are you looking for "a few good storms?" Well, there are no good storms when you're out on the water. On the other hand, lots of Ohioans spend a little time up on Lake Erie each year. Some spend a lot of time on that Great Lake. For those who do, here are a couple of important terms you should be aware of. A small craft advisory is issued when winds reach up to 39 miles per hour (mph), and the resulting waves may threaten boaters. And you can just forget about a day on the lake when a gale warning is in effect. The National Weather Service issues gale warnings when winds reach between 39 and 54 mph. Holy Dramamine®, Batman!

METEOROLOGIST

Yes, believe it or not, we do actually go to school to do what we do. We're scientists who study the atmosphere and all its phenomena. When you get right down to it, meteorology is mostly math and science. You can study it at many of Ohio's great universities, including The Ohio State University and Ohio University.

There are all sorts of uses for meteorology (and meteorologists) including research, commercial forecasting, radio, television, agriculture, business, hydrology, and aviation.

METEOROLOGY

In a nutshell, meteorology is the study of our atmosphere... the weather. As you're no doubt aware, and remind me from time to time, it's not an exact science. (Frankly, I don't think it ever will be.)

Forecasters will likely always deal in probabilities and percentages. After all, the system we're trying to predict is so complicated and erratic that it almost seems as though it has moods that make it work one way on one day and differently on another.

Despite the fact that I get lots of calls during meteor showers, they never taught us about these kinds of showers back at Ohio State. Sure, the words are similar, but for frozen balls of rock, ice, and gas shooting through outer space (where there is no weather, *per se*) please consult an astronomer. (see **Stargazing**)

The word "meteorology" probably dates back well over 2000 years, to the time of the great Greek scholar and philosopher Aristotle. Way back in about 350 B.C., Aristotle gathered all his weather-related information, explanations, and ruminations into a magnum opus entitled *Meteorologica*. Clearly ahead of his time, he hit many of the basic principles of our atmosphere right on the head. However, there were other cases where interesting speculation, such as the one about living in a spherical universe, significantly missed the mark.

Still, he may very well have coined the word we so casually throw about today. In Greek, the word "meteor" means "of the sky," while "logy" means "study of" or "discourse" referring to communication through writing or speech.

MIXED BAG

"Cop out. Cop out," cry Dave Kaylor and Andrea Cambern, my co-anchors at 5:00 p.m. on WBNS-10TV in Columbus, Ohio, from across the studio. Oh sure, I admit it, this one covers a lot of ground! But Ohio is the classic "wait five minutes and it'll change" state. And sometimes in the course of a single day, we run the gamut weatherwise: periods of sun, clouds, rain, snow, wind... all in a twelve-hour period. Other ways to describe those kinds of days include: potpourri, changeable, variably cloudy, and just plain weird.

NATIONAL CENTERS FOR ENVIRONMENTAL PREDICTION (NCEP)

Located near Washington D.C., the NCEP, is where all the government's giant number-crunching super-computers analyze data and spit out the myriad maps and charts that we use in making our forecasts. These same charts are used by meteorologists all over the country. Since weather forecasting is a numbers game, all physics and calculus, these big-brained beasts make it possible for us to predict the weather before it happens, which seems to be what people expect. After all, any fool could give you a good forecast for yesterday! My accuracy there is 100%!

But think about it. If meteorologists everywhere are using the same basic information in preparing our forecasts, why don't we all say the same thing when it gets down to whether you should pack an umbrella tomorrow? The answer: experience and insight. It's our job to analyze what those computers are telling us and decide whether the computer models making the call are right or wrong. As far as TV weather forecasting goes, it's then up to you to decide who you trust the most. I have a suggestion… then again, I'm kind of partial!

NATIONAL HURRICANE CENTER (NHC)

The NHC keeps its eyes and ears open during the tropical weather season. The NHC, located in Miami, Florida, is responsible for keeping a constant watch on tropical cyclones over the Atlantic Ocean, Caribbean Sea, Gulf of Mexico, and the eastern Pacific Ocean from May 15th through November 30th. The meteorologists at the NHC track hurricane development and movement from the earliest stages in an effort to issue timely watches and warnings to protect life and property.

NATIONAL OCEANIC AND ATMOSPHERIC ADMINISTRATION (NOAA)

Better known as NOAA, (pronounced Noah, like the guy with the ark; besides, that way we're on a first name basis), this organization is, by far, the largest employer of civilian meteorologists. About two-thirds of NOAA's meteorologists work for the National Weather Service. Most of the rest are involved in meteorological research.

NOAA WEATHER RADIO

Lots of people have these. They're small, usually battery operated radios, that provide weather information 24 hours a day. Your nearest National Weather Service office provides recorded hourly conditions, forecasts, as well as various warning services. In fact, some of these radios have built-in alarms that go off in the event of threatening weather. There are a number of transmitter sites in Ohio, broadcasting on a variety of special FM frequencies.

NOAA Weather Radio Frequencies

Akron:	162.400 MHz	Lima:	162.400 MHz
Bridgeport:	162.525 MHz	Otway:	162.525 MHz
Cleveland:	162.550 MHz	Sandusky:	162.400 MHz
Columbus:	162.550 MHz	Toledo:	162.550 MHz
Dayton:	162.475 MHz	Youngstown:	162.525 MHz
High Hill:	162.475 MHz		

NOAA weather radios can usually be found at your neighborhood electronics store. You can also often find the signal on some local cable TV channels. The idea behind the service is to provide on-demand weather information and immediate warnings. The responsibility for these services in Ohio is handled by the National Weather Service Offices in Cleveland and Wilmington, Ohio, Pittsburgh, Pennsylvania, and Charleston, West Virginia.

The NOAA weather radio network is growing. A new transmitter, serving some 228,000 new households in southern Ohio went on-line in January 2001.

NATIONAL WEATHER SERVICE (NWS)

A division of the United States Department of Commerce, the National Weather Service is part of the National Oceanic and Atmospheric Administration, NOAA (see above). The NWS, which has been consolidating its operations under a massive modernization program, is charged with providing the best possible forecasts as well as issuing timely severe weather watches and warnings. The meteorologists at the NWS use satellite information, state of the art NEXRAD systems, automated reporting stations, a spotter's network, and super-speed computers in making their forecasts.

The NWS' main forecasting office for Ohio is in Cleveland, but the various watch and warning duties for most of central Ohio are handled by the Wilmington, Ohio, office. Warnings for parts of east central Ohio come out of the Pittsburgh, Pennsylvania, office, while warnings for southeast Ohio are issued by the NWS in Charleston, West Virginia.

The mission of the NWS is to protect the life and property of U.S. citizens from natural disasters by issuing timely warnings and forecasts for hurricanes, tornadoes, floods, winter and summer storms, and all manners of severe and extreme weather.

NEPHELOCOCCYGIA

I thought meteorology was tough to spell! Question: Have you
ever looked up at the clouds and said, "that one looks like a
dinosaur," or "those clouds look like a castle in the sky?" Can you
believe there's a name for this? (Sounds more like a diagnosis.)
Nephelococcygia is the act of "seeing things" in the clouds. Who
knew? Try throwing that word into your next conversation! By
the way, if you do this, does that make you a Nephelococcygist?
I hope my co-anchors never have to introduce me like that!

NOR' EASTER

A nor'easter (northeaster) is a powerful winter storm that roars up
the east coast, producing high winds, heavy rain, and pounding
surf along the coast and heavy snow and gusty winds inland. A
nor'easter forms when an upper level storm approaches from the
Midwest and encounters a strong surface low pressure system
with a sharp temperature contrast over the northeast coast. The
storm pulls in moisture from the ocean as well as cold northern
air. The result is heavy rain and snow, strong winds, waves, and
coastal erosion. The storm gets its name from the abundant rain or
snow that's drawn in from the Atlantic Ocean on the heels of the
northeast wind.

NORMAL

Who is to say what "normal" is? Besides, normal changes with
time! But for meteorological purposes, normal refers to "typical"
or "average" weather for a particular place at a particular time of
year. Normals are based on 30-year averages, so they do, in fact,
change over time as our environment gradually changes.

Just to give you an example, the average daily high and low for
the month of January in Columbus, Ohio, are 37°F and 22°F. By
July, the average daily high and low for the month have

skyrocketed to 85°F and 65°F! For those of us living in the Midwest or Great Lakes region, these are pretty typical seasonal variations. But if you lived in Quito, Equador, the "land of perpetual spring," this would seem extreme in the extreme! The average daily high for the month in Quito only varies between 70–73°F, all year long! And the swing in the average daily low is also just a few measly degrees, between 44°F and 47°F. Not bad, I'd say. You'd always know what to pack for a visit.

If you want to talk extremes, here are a couple of examples. What would you think about a place where the average daily high, over the course of a year, varies by 120 degrees and the average low changes by 111 degrees? Of course, it's one of the coldest places on Earth, but if you like variety, you might want to try Verkhoyansk in Siberia. June and July aren't bad. The average daily high for those months climbs as high as 66°F, while the average low for those months can be as mild as 47°F–48°F. Not bad. But you might want to think about going south for the winter. Why, you ask? Here's why. By January, the average daily high for the month is -54°F! Can you say throw an extra tree on the fire? Fortunately, temperatures don't drop all that much more at night. Still, the average daily low in January is -63°F. Hey, that's only 11 degrees cooler than the high. Have you winterized your igloo yet?

In Columbus, Ohio, we average a little more than 38 inches of precipitation each year. By contrast, if you lived in Las Vegas, Nevada, like I did before moving here, the average rainfall is just over four inches (about 10 times less than Columbus). If that's still not dry enough, you might want to think about Thule, Greenland. That's another cold place. The average precipitation there is about two and one-half inches. And most of that is from snowfall. Still too damp? Then Aswan, Egypt, is the place for you! Average monthly rainfall: zero. Average yearly rainfall: zero. (Not a good place to set up an umbrella franchise.)

Do you like it warm and dry? Try Riyadh, Saudi Arabia. Sure, it rains a little, almost three and one-quarter inches a year, but it rarely rains a drop between the end of May and January! What's more, the average daily high between May and January is a healthy 96°F. Between June and August, it's 107°F.

OK, maybe you like things a little wetter. There's a little place in South America you might like. It's called Andagoya, Columbia. There, average monthly rainfall is over 20 inches. The climate is warm but, as you might expect, fairly humid. Normal highs only budge about three degrees, from 88°F–90°F. The average daily low, however, changes even less. From 74°F–75°F. Still not soggy enough? Try Cherrapunji, India. It's one of the three wettest places in the world. The average yearly rainfall can exceed 425 inches! And no, it doesn't rain there all the time. The average rainfall in December is only about a half inch. June, however, tends to be a little damp. Let's put it this way, you'd better take a few umbrellas. The average rainfall in June is over 106 inches. Bad hair days galore!

OCEANS/THE OCEAN ABOVE

First things first. Oceans are huge bodies of salt water. And while it might not be obvious, oceans can have a major impact on our weather. In fact, the oceans and the air have a lot in common. They are inexorably interconnected and are a prime example of how the entire global environment is intertwined.

Let's take a closer look. Right off the bat, both are fluids. What's more, both have waves. And both are great transporters of heat and moisture (see **El Niño** and **La Niña**). And both can have a major impact on life on Earth. In essence, the oceans and the air make up the Earth's thermostat.

These similarities are the focus of a Columbus, Ohio, COSI exhibit, "The Ocean Above, Our Global Weather."

OHIO vs. THE WORLD

Many of us tell ourselves that we live in Ohio because of the seasons. Sure, we all have our favorites, but Ohio has got them all: winter, spring, summer, and fall. It makes my life more interesting.

But, let's say you like consistency, something the weather is not particularly famous for here in central Ohio. You might want to consider Guyana on the Atlantic coast of South America. The normal high, year-round, only varies between 84°F–87°F. The normal low hovers between 74°F–76°F all year. Of course, if that appeals to you, I must warn you that it rains a lot in the summer and is humid all year, too. By the same token, it can't be much fun for local TV weather guys compared to our "wait five minutes and it will change" weather.

Now, if you prefer even more variety than the Buckeye state offers, you may want to think about Mongolia, in the heart of Asia. In Ulaanbaatar in January, for example, the normal high is -2°F. The normal low is -26°F. Occasional (brace yourself) the mercury drops to -50°F, at which point, mercury freezes. Nippy!

Still, by June, the normal high has rebounded to a healthy 71°F. That's a swing of 97 degrees! Still, I'm guessing that winters there get a little long. It doesn't rain much either, just about five inches a year. (At least it's a dry cold.)

Here's another possibility. In the coastal city of Douala, Cameroon, in central Africa, the rainy season runs from June to September. Doesn't sound too bad, right? The catch is, they average 20–30 inches of rain each of those months. If that isn't bad enough, Cameroon Peak is one of three spots in the entire world that averages over 400 inches of rain every year. Here's a tip: pack your umbrella.

New Zealand sounds nice. The climate there is described as healthy, pleasant, and non-hazardous. In Auckland, on the North Island, normal lows vary between 40°F–60°F. Normal highs range from 56°F–73°F. In my book, that's pretty tolerable. It is a little rainy, though, and some of the mountains feature year-round glaciers.

I guess this goes to prove that there's a little something out there for everyone in this great big world of ours. And sure, you can shop around, but there are definitely some nice things about Ohio's weather, don't you think?

OMEGA BLOCK

Sounds like the name of a good spy novel, eh? Then again, maybe it's a terrific row of fraternities over at The Ohio State University. But truth be told, it's another part of the wonderful world of weather. A good subtitle might be "stuck in a rut" because that's exactly what happens when an omega block sets up.

An omega block occurs, mainly in summer, when a large dome of high pressure sets up, causing the air flow pattern over the country to resemble the Greek letter omega (Ω) on a pressure chart. If you are under the dome, the result can be day after day of sunshine and, probably, abnormally warm temperatures. Since the air in this region is generally falling, and the winds are typically light, there's very little air movement, and the air can stagnate causing pollution problems and lingering haze. (The sky may look more brown than blue.)

If you are in one of the dips on either side of the dome, it can be exactly the opposite: day after day of stormy or unsettled weather. The omega block prevents the normal west to east movement of storms around the country. As a result, the forecast can, for weeks on end, be monotonously the same.

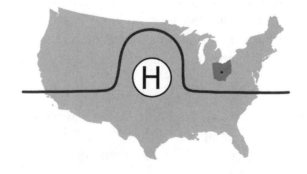

OZONE LAYER

There are two types of ozone… the good kind and the bad kind. The latter is a pollutant that exists near the ground. Ozone is a colorless gas made up of three oxygen atoms. It forms near the ground when exhaust from cars and other motors reacts with the heat and oxygen in the air.

The hotter the day, the more ozone created. Many metropolitan areas issue ozone alerts when stagnant air becomes a health risk. Ozone alerts are becoming increasingly common here in Ohio.

The "good" ozone is found way up in our atmosphere, between 9 and 13 miles high. The reason this ozone is so important is that it acts like a filter against incoming ultraviolet radiation. Without the protective ozone layer, there would be an increase in skin cancer.

The fact that "holes" have appeared in the ozone layer in recent years have led to bans on things like chlorofluorocarbons (CFCs) that, over time, cause this protective ozone to break down.

PARTLY CLOUDY vs PARTLY SUNNY

When a meteorologist speaks these words, confusion "rains." (If you'll pardon the expression.) The question is, if you like sunshine, which of these is more your kind of day? Over-whelmingly, when I ask this question, the answer comes up partly sunny. The reason? People don't hear the word "partly." They only hear the words cloudy or sunny. (Perhaps they're only *partly* listening!)

For all intents and purposes, these terms are often used as meaning the same thing: a day that's neither completely cloudy nor completely sunny. But look at it this way. If the sky is partly cloudy, what's the rest of it? Conversely, if the sky is partly sunny, what's the rest of it? See where I'm heading?

Partly cloudy or partly sunny?

It's all relative. On a partly cloudy day, the clouds never completely cover-up the Sun. But they can obscure 30% to 60% of the sky. On a partly sunny day, clouds cover more than 60% of the sky but not more than 80%. If that happens, we move on to mostly cloudy. Follow me? ("Well, stop following me or I'll have you arrested," as Groucho Marx used to say.)

I prefer more descriptive phrases like "a mix of sun and clouds," "increasing clouds," or "clouds giving way to sunshine." On those changeable Ohio days, the term "variable clouds" comes in very handy. That way, people seem to be less disappointed if a day fails to live up to personal expectations. Besides, what do you call those days when it's six of one thing, half a dozen of another? Keep in mind, a day's forecast is supposed to take in the entire day in just a few short words.

POTHOLES

Do you remember thinking, just before the front end of your car vanished, and you saw your hubcaps flying off in either direction, "it's just a puddle?" Well, you were wrong. It was actually one of our famous alignment wrecking, home-grown, bigger than a bread box Ohio potholes! These are especially common in climates known for changeable weather. (A mixed bag?)

Potholes are created during those freeze-thaw cycles that are so common in the eastern half of the United States. It all starts when water under the pavement freezes. As water freezes, it expands, pushing down soil under the pavement. When the ice melts, there's now a cavity left beneath the surface of the road. As cars move over the pavement, it frequently collapses into the cavity leaving (you guessed it) POTHOLES! Potholes are so common and costly that many cities have formed pothole patrols and even have pothole hotlines for reporting trouble spots.

PRECIPITATION

Precipitation is moisture, whether frozen or liquid, that falls (precipitates) from clouds.

When talking about duration, we use terms like brief, occasional, intermittent, and frequent. When talking about intensity, we use words like very light, light, heavy, and very heavy. Guess what? Although we sometimes seem to use these in a general fashion, each of these terms has a very specific definition.

Very Light means less than 0.01" per hour.

Light means 0.01" to 0.10" per hour.

Moderate means 0.10" to 0.30" per hour.

Heavy means more than 0.30" per hour.

PROBABILITY OF PRECIPITATION (POP)

Here's another one of those forecasting expressions that's more trouble than it's worth.

The probability of precipitation (POP) is that almost proverbial "30% chance of rain." What does that really mean? Will it rain 30% of the time? Will it rain over just 30% of the viewing area? Or, are raindrops just a third of their normal size? In my mind, at least, the old "30% chance" equates to "rain doesn't look likely, but I can't quite rule it out, either." I'm tempted to call it the "cover your you know what forecast."

Here's the "official" National Weather Service definition. The probability of precipitation is the likelihood of occurrence, expressed as a percentage, of precipitation at any given point in the forecast area. There are two components of this: the expression of uncertainty and the equivalent areal coverage.

Probability of Precipitation	Expression of Uncertainty	Equivalent Areal Coverage
0%	None used	None Used
10%	Slight Chance	Isolated or Few
20%	Slight Chance	Widely Scattered
30-50%	Chance	Scattered
60-70%	Likely	Numerous
80-100%	None Used	None Used

QUANTITATIVE PRECIPITATION FORECAST

For whatever reason, amounts seem much more important when the forecast calls for snow, as opposed to rain. With rain, the main questions are "when" and "how long." But for snow, the questions are "when" and "how much." Either way, it's all the same to those of us who make the forecasts. All precipitation — rain or snow — is based upon its liquid equivalent (water content).

If we're talking rain, hey, water is water. But the forecast is much trickier when we're talking snow. When predicting snow, it's the meteorologist's job to figure out the liquid-to-frozen water ratio and whether there will be any kind of transition period along the way. Sometimes this is a very fine line. A difference of a degree or two can really mess up a forecast.

QUASI-STATIONARY FRONT

That's long-winded weather jargon for a front that's not really moving or whose relative position is changing very slowly between one observation and the next. Stationary fronts, more than likely, will eventually move one way or the other, the forecasting trick is determining when and where. Easier said than done. This too can really wreak havoc on a forecast.

RADAR

Radar stands for **RA**dio **D**etection **A**nd **R**anging. The government just loves acronyms. That's when you take an abbreviation and make a word out of it. But what does a radar do? Well, think of it this way. If you throw a rubber ball into a crowd of people, it's bound to hit someone. When it does, it bounces back. That's the basic principle behind radar.

A radar sends out a short, narrow beam of energy, called a pulse. The radar then kicks back and listens for waves that are reflected back or scattered back toward the receiver. The amount of time that passes between when the pulse went out and when it's reflected back to the antenna tells how far away the rain is.

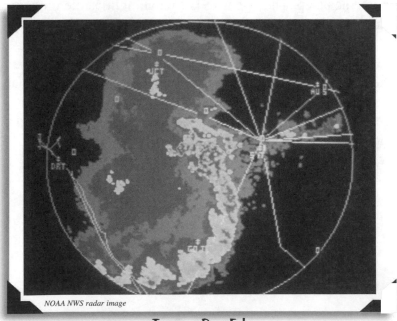

NOAA NWS radar image

Texas — Bow Echo

The amount of scattering really depends on the size of the rain drops (or snow flakes) and the wavelength of the radio waves being transmitted. Keep in mind, tiny little raindrops and ice crystals reflect very little energy back toward the radar. Only the most sensitive radars, like the new Next Generation Doppler Radars (NEXRADs) or Live Dual Doppler 10 Radar, can effectively pick up and track light snow. And that brings up the second function of a radar… to track the movement of precipitation. Radars give meteorologists the time they need to warn the public of approaching storms.

RADIATIONAL COOLING

During the day, the Earth's surface heats up as it absorbs the Sun's rays. But at night, especially clear nights, the Earth quickly loses its heat by radiating it back into the atmosphere.

Like basic economics, it's all a matter of deficits and surpluses. While the Sun is shining, the Earth's surface experiences a net gain and heats up. The opposite is true at night as the outgoing radiation leads to a net loss and a cooling at the surface.

Fun Fact: It's because of radiational cooling that we can have frost in the morning even though the official temperature may be above freezing. The official temperature is taken by a thermometer in a screened enclosure several feet above the surface. The actual surface temperature may indeed be cooler due to the pace at which it radiates heat back into the atmosphere.

RAIN & SHOWERS

"Rain, rain go away. Come again some other day." "April showers bring May flowers." Both are an integral part of weather folklore and Ohio forecasts. And in both cases, you'd better grab an umbrella. But there is a difference. Rain implies a certain steadiness to the falling moisture. It tends to develop slowly, to last longer, and it often covers a wide area. Rainfall totals tend to be higher than those from intermittent showers.

By contrast, showers come and go. Rain that comes from showers tends to change in intensity quickly with sudden stops and starts. And precipitation from showers tends to be pretty hit and miss. Cloud cover also varies greatly in showery weather, while there's a more consistent low overcast on rainy days. When talking about showers, we typically use words like intermittent, occasional, or scattered to describe their occurrence.

Rain, rain, go away.

Technically speaking, rain is the name given to all liquid precipitation other than drizzle. The smallest raindrops are 0.5 millimeters in diameter (0.02 inches). They are only limited in size due to the fact that drops bigger than 0.20 inches tend to be unstable and break up into smaller droplets as they fall. Like everything else, meteorologists have divided rainfall into several categories. Light rain falls at rates of less than 0.1 inch per hour, moderate rain falls at 0.11–0.30 inches per hour and rain is called heavy if it falls at a rate greater than 0.30 inches per hour.

Say that again… in English! OK, the very smallest raindrops, which almost float, fall to earth very slowly, at the rate of about one mile per hour (mph). The biggest raindrops can fall at just under 20 mph. The largest of these rarely exceed a quarter of an inch in diameter. If they ever got much bigger, the motion of the air around these massive drops would tend to shatter them well before splash down.

RAINBOW

One of the prettiest sights in nature. Wordsworth once said, "My heart leaps up when I behold a rainbow in the sky." Rainbows are circular arcs composed of beautiful bands of color surrounding the point opposite in the sky from the Moon or the Sun. You need two things to make a rainbow: bright light and moisture in the air. The spectacular effect is created by the light being refracted and reflected by the raindrops or other moisture in the air.

Of course, like all weather phenomena, rainbows have a technical side. The main rainbow has an angular radius of about 42 degrees. (Sounds like geometry, doesn't it?) And because of the way light is "bent" when passing through the raindrop, the red is on the inside and blue and violet are on the outside. Sometimes the effect really gets carried away! Occasionally, you get a secondary rainbow. It appears at a 50 degree angular radius, and the colors are reversed, with violet and blue on the inside and red on the outside! If you're really lucky, you sometimes even get a third rainbow. The colors are reversed again, matching the first rainbow. Even four rainbows are possible at a time... but typically, you'll only see the first one or two. Still, wouldn't four be a sight?

Folklore: "Rainbow afternoon, good weather comes soon."

More Folklore: If a rainbow is broken in two or three places, or if only half of it is visible, rainy weather can be expected for as many days as there are breaks!

RELATIVE HUMIDITY

You've probably heard the old expression "it's all relative." However, the speaker probably wasn't referring to humidity. But the question remains: relative to what? The answer is: relative to temperature and relative to how much water can evaporate into the air at a given temperature. In a nutshell, it's a measure of how much water the air can hold at a given temperature. On a daily basis, there's typically a large swing in the relative humidity. It's highest in the morning when the temperature is typically at its lowest. On those occasions when the temperature and the dew point meet in the morning (100% relative humidity), dew forms.

Relative humidity is measured using a device called a hygrometer. The oldest and most widely used hygrometer uses human hair as its main component. That's right: human hair! After all, organic substances like hair are very good at absorbing moisture. On humid days, the hair expands, moving a pointer which indicates the relative humidity. I guess this explains why humid days are often "bad hair days."

Fun Fact: Based on annual averages, portions of coastal Washington state, northern Oregon, and western Maine have the highest relative humidities in the United States, while the interiors of southern California and southern Nevada have the lowest.

Question: Can the relative humidity go above 100%? You bet! Inside clouds, air can be supersaturated, with a relative humidity approaching 102%. This is one of the causes behind the growth of cloud droplets. (This one may come in handy if you're ever playing trivia.)

RIDGE

We all know that "R-R-R-RUFFLES® HAVE R-R-RIDGES™". But did you know that our atmosphere does too? When you hear us talking about ridges on TV, that's usually a good thing. You see, a ridge is a long area of high pressure. Air typically "falls" under a high pressure ridge (not to be confused with "folding" under pressure), which brings fair skies or nice weather.

SEASONAL AFFECTIVE DISORDER (SAD)

Also called the winter blues, SAD is a real disorder that affects real people when the days grow short during the winter months. Among the symptoms are problems sleeping, overeating and weight gain, depression, family problems, fatigue, even physical ailments like joint and stomach pains, as well as a tendency to get sick more often.

You may have noticed there's a good reason why Ohio's not called "the Sunshine State," especially in the winter. January skies in Columbus are clear just over 14% of the time. Well, as with most things related to the weather and real estate, it's all about location, location, location.

The same thing that makes extreme northeast Ohio part of the snow belt, makes Columbus and the rest of central Ohio, "cloud city" during the winter. Cold air coming across Lake Erie dumps snow in Ashtabula, Geauga, and Lake counties, while pumping lake effect clouds over much of the remainder of the state.

If you're a sufferer, trust me, you're not alone. Close to ten million people a year are thought to be in the same boat, though specific diagnosis can be difficult. Even animals feel it!

The real problem is that SAD sufferers have lost their rhythm, the body's built-in clock that tells you when to fall asleep at night and when to wake up in the morning. Technically speaking, the body's pineal gland reacts to the darkness by secreting the hormone melatonin, which helps the body relax and sleep.

Daylight, in turn, triggers the gland to shut down production and lets the body wake up. This is a much tougher order given winter's shorter days.

Light therapy is the traditional remedy for SAD. But this involves buying a light box and spending a good part of an hour each day letting your body soak in these artificial rays. Research on other treatments continues. Other helpful remedies include regular exercise and morning walks. These you can do on your own, but if the winter blues make you SAD enough to consider light therapy, you really should consult your physician.

SEVERE THUNDERSTORMS

Severe thunderstorms are highly efficient "machines," with strong updrafts and the ability to last hours longer than garden-variety thunderstorms. Severe thunderstorms may produce large hail, lightning, high winds, torrential rain, even tornadoes.

Like everything, the term "severe thunderstorm" has a very explicit definition. A thunderstorm is severe if it produces at least 58-miles-per-hour winds, hail that's $3/4$ inches or larger, or if funnel clouds or tornadoes develop.

SEVERE THUNDERSTORM WARNING

A severe thunderstorm warning is issued when severe weather has already developed and has been reported by spotters or indicated by radar. Warnings are statements of imminent danger and cover relatively small areas near and ahead of the approaching severe weather.

122

SEVERE THUNDERSTORM WATCH

A severe thunderstorm watch is issued when conditions exist that could produce a severe thunderstorm. There are no guarantees. A watch identifies a relatively large area where such storms might develop, typically about 140 miles wide by about 200 miles long. Watches are usually issued before any severe weather has developed.

SLEET

How do you feel about bouncing balls of ice? In a nutshell, that's what sleet is. Sleet is solid grains of ice that form when rain freezes before reaching the ground. Not only do these little ice pellets bounce, they can actually accumulate, like snow, covering the ground by as much as a couple of inches!

SMOG

This is not one of my favorites. Fortunately, it's not a huge problem in central Ohio. The word comes from combining two other words: smoke and fog. Oddly enough, smog isn't either one of these. It's produced by a complex reaction of pollutant gases and sunlight. Smog is very "common" in cities like Los Angeles and Denver.

SNOW

As Ohioans, we know snow! And during the winter months, there are lots of snow related terms that creep into our forecasts. For example, snow comes in pellets, flakes, flurries, showers, storms, and squalls. There are also heavy snow watches and warnings, blowing snow, drifting snow, and accumulating snow. And don't forget snow cover, snow line, snowfall, even "snow days." Folks, that's a lot of snow!

Simply put, snow is frozen, crystalline precipitation. These crystals collect to form snowflakes that grow into many beautiful shapes and patterns. And, it's true, no two are alike. But I'm quite sure that doesn't matter in the slightest as you're shoveling tons of these crystals off your drive-way or when you're stuck in a crystal related traffic jam.

Here are some average seasonal snowfalls for some Ohio cities:

Columbus	28 inches
Zanesville	28 inches
Portsmouth	24 inches
Athens	24 inches
Dayton	25 inches
Toledo	35 inches

Of course, there's nothing more beautiful to a kid, or a teacher for that matter, than to wake up to a fresh blanket of snow on Friday morning, necessitating a "snow day" because the school is buried somewhere beneath a huge drift. I guess it's all a case of perspective.

SNOW ADVISORY

Just to make things more complicated, here's a term that means different things in different parts of Ohio. In central Ohio, a snow advisory is issued by the National Weather Service when one to three inches of snow are expected to fall within 24 hours. Likewise, the term heavy snow refers to four inches or more, within a 12-hour period, or six inches or more, over a 24-hour period. But just to show that it's all relative, a snow advisory is issued for northern Ohio when three to five inches are expected within the next 12 hours, while heavy snow refers to six inches or more within the next 12–24 hours.

SNOW BELT

Ohio's snow belt consists of Cuyahoga County (east of Cleveland), as well as Ashtabula, Geauga, and Lake counties. It also extends into western Pennsylvania. Does someone up there not like these counties? Not at all. It's simply a case of geography, which plays a big role in determining a place's weather. In this case, we're talking about an area just east of Lake Erie. And, since the jet stream and the prevailing winds move west to east, there's often cold air blowing across the lake. These winds pick up moisture, freeze it, convert it to snow, and rudely dump it on the snow belt. As a result, these locations literally get "belted" by heavy snowfall during the winter months. The annual seasonal snowfall for extreme northeast Ohio is more than 100 inches. The funny thing is, it can be snowing up a storm across the snow belt and can be absolutely quiet across the rest of Ohio. Seems like a good argument for not moving to the snow belt!

SNOW BURN

Have you ever gone spring skiing? I did… once. And I thought I must have picked "Mimes on the Mountain" day. It seemed like everyone but me was wearing a "white face." As it turns out, they were all wearing heavy duty sunscreen. Bottom line: it was the worst sunburn I ever had.

Actually, it was a snow burn, caused by sunlight being reflected off the snow. Take my advice, don't underestimate the strength of cool weather sunshine!

Don't forget the sunscreen!

SNOW COVER

The amount of snow on the ground can have a dramatic impact on our winter weather. Would you believe that, as cold as it feels to the touch, snow actually keeps the ground warmer in the winter? It's true. The snow helps trap the Earth's heat. That way, even

126

with sub-zero temperatures, the ground can remain unfrozen as long as it's covered by a thick blanket of insulating snow. (Just ask a gravedigger.)

On the other hand, snow cover can have a very negative impact on the temperature as we perceive it. For one thing, snow reflects sunlight away from the surface, not allowing it to warm up as it would otherwise. A heavy covering of snow can have a 5–10 degree impact on our daytime high temperature, something which our computer forecast models fail to take into account. As meteorologists, it's our job to factor these things in, even when the computers can't.

FYI: Snow covered roads are slow to melt because of the way snow reflects the sunlight. But, if the snow is dirty or covered with sand, both of which can better absorb the suns heat, snow will melt away much more quickly. You may also notice that snow next to trees and fences seems to melt much faster than snow in the middle of your yard. Well, that's because trees and wooden fences absorb the Sun's heat and radiate it outward, melting the adjacent snow.

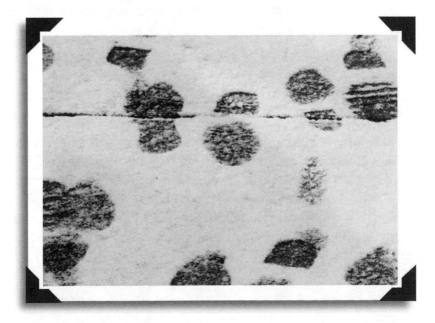

SNOW EMERGENCY

There are those who believe that any time it snows... it's an emergency. But like so many things, there's an OFFICIAL definition. The sheriff's department in each county has the authority to declare a snow emergency for the purpose of "preserving the public peace." Best of all, snow emergencies come in a variety of shapes and sizes.

Levels of a Snow Emergency

Level 1: Drive carefully. Roads are icy and hazardous with blowing and drifting snow.

Level 2: Drive only if you think it's necessary. Roads are hazardous with blowing and drifting snow. Contact your employer to see if you should go to work.

Level 3: Driving is a no-no. In fact, you may be arrested if you do! Roads are closed to non-emergency vehicles. No one should be out unless absolutely necessary. Employees should contact work to see if they should report. What are the odds?

SNOW SHOVELING

Oh, my aching back! How many times have you felt that way after shoveling the walk or driveway after a big snow storm? Well, guess what. You're not a wimp. There's a good reason for being a little bent out of shape. Did you know that the average shovel-full of snow weighs about seven pounds. (Not counting the shovel!) That's about the same as having a gallon of milk on the end of your shovel.

And get this: shoveling a driveway that measures 20 feet by 20 feet, means you have to shovel about 4 tons of snow. That's equal to the weight of a pair of hippos. Wouldn't it be great if you could just ask them to move?

SNOW SQUALL

A snow squall is an intense fall of accumulating snow often accompanied by windy conditions. You see a lot of these squalls during the winter months in the snow belt. Squalls are common along the eastern shores of all the Great Lakes because cold air blows across the surface of the lake, picks up moisture, then dumps it as "lake-effect" snow.

SOLSTICE

Occurring twice a year, the solstices are the point at which the Sun is furthest from the equator and the days and nights are most unequal. The winter solstice occurs on or around December 21st, while the summer solstice falls on or around June 21st.

SPRING

Perhaps the most popular season of all, spring signals a rebirth in nature, as winter snows melt away and trees and flowers begin to bloom. Meteorologically speaking, spring consists of March, April, and May. Paradoxically, spring is also the beginning of tornado season, thus making it a season with some of the most pleasant AND most violent days. (see **Vernal Equinox**; **Buzzards of Hinckley**)

Spring has caused many to wax poetic.

The nicest thing about the promise of spring is that sooner or later she'll have to keep it.
Mark Beltaire

No one thinks of winter when the grass is green.
Rudyard Kipling

April is the cruellest month, breeding Lilacs out of the dead land, mixing memory and desire, stirring dull roots with spring rain.
T. S. Eliot

No winter lasts forever, no spring skips its turn. April is a promise that May is bound to keep, and we know it.
Hal Borland

STARGAZING

I get calls about all types of astronomical phenomena. And while I'm fascinated by everything that happens in the sky, I must admit that the stars are a little outside my realm of expertise. Fortunately, we have a stellar resource in our community if you have stars in your eyes.

Perkins Observatory is located on the campus of Ohio Wesleyan University in Delaware. Calling itself "The Place for Space," the observatory offers a whole host of programs for the astronomically inclined.

The observatory's history is equally fascinating. Named for it's creator, Ohio Wesleyan professor Hiram Mills Perkins, the telescope itself was not completed until 1931. At the time, the telescope with a 69-inch mirror was the 3rd largest in the world.

At that time, the observatory had one of the best astronomical libraries in the world, and astronomers from all over the globe regularly visited the facility.

Unfortunately, several factors hurt the observatory. The biggest problem, ironically, was its central Ohio location. There was too much "light pollution" from Columbus and Delaware, the elevation here was too low, and central Ohio weather patterns were not conducive to clear skies.

In 1961, the big telescope was removed and taken to an observatory in Arizona, and subsequently replaced with a much smaller one. In 1999, after an almost 40-year absence, the original mirror, which just happened to be the first large telescope mirror ever cast in the Western Hemisphere, was returned to the observatory where it remains on display today.

For more information on the observatory's programs, hours, and events, you can call 740-363-1257. You can also find lots of great stuff on the observatory's web site: http://www.perkins-observatory.org.

STATIC ELECTRICITY

Ouch! I'm talking about the little, or not so little, shocks you get after you've shuffled your feet across the carpet, especially on a dry, winter day. A static electric charge builds up on your shoes and clothing because of the low indoor relative humidity. Much like lightning, the spark is caused by a build up of positive and negative charges. And the results can be shocking! Each inch of spark represents a potential difference of 40,000 volts!

STORM CHASERS

The kamikazes of our profession. Their goal: "To boldly go where no one has gone before." More modestly put, they'd like to put a Doppler radar inside a tornado or, at the very least, take a picture at point blank range! For most of us, that's a little too close for comfort. But in the pursuit of science and discovery, is any risk too great? These folks don't seem to think so. Prime real estate for these thrill-seekers are places like Texas, Kansas, and Oklahoma on a hot summer afternoon. For those of you interested in meteorology, but afraid that the scientific life might be a little dull and academic, then storm chasing might just be your calling.

As for the tornado chasers, most are more detectives than daredevils. And believe it or not, the key to this "sport" is patience. Storm season is short, and the odds are long. After all, predicting exactly where a tornado will appear is extremely difficult. But it's even tougher to get in close, get the picture, and get out alive! What a rush! But that's exactly what happened in 1995 with Project Vortex. The outcome of these first hand observations cast new light on these amazingly violent storms.

Of course, when you want real first hand observations of the winds within a tornado, you'll have to consult TOTO, and I don't mean Dorothy's dog. TOTO stands for **TO**table **T**ornado **O**bservatory. A TOTO contains portable wind sensing equipment designed to be dropped in the path of an approaching tornado. Anyone for a good game of chicken?

STORM PREDICTION CENTER (SPC)

Located in Norman, Oklahoma, the center maintains a staff of meteorologists whose job it is to pay close attention to changing weather conditions around the country. (Especially those patterns which might produce or sustain any type of severe weather.) It is the SPC's job, year-round, to alert other weather related agencies and the public of the potential for severe weather by issuing watches and warnings.

The SPC, formerly the National Severe Storms Forecast Center, is a special agency within the National Weather Service. It was established because of the high incidence of severe weather across the eastern two-thirds of the United States. The SPC describes its mission as enhancing the National Weather Service's capabilities for providing accurate and timely forecasts and warnings of hazardous weather events.

STRAIGHT-LINE WINDS

These are strong thunderstorm winds that can blow down homes and buildings, leaving behind a path of destruction much like that of a tornado. In fact, we usually get reports of tornadoes after straight-line winds rip through a neighborhood. For one thing, the devastation is very similar and is often accompanied by a roar that mimics the sound of a tornado.

Straight-line winds are caused by strong downdrafts from thunderstorms, called downbursts or microbursts. The actual burst is a fast-falling rush of cold air, usually under heavy rainfall, that hits the ground and fans out in a powerful gust front. In extreme cases, these winds can hit 125 miles per hour! (Comparable to a Category 3 hurricane or an F2 tornado!) Although damage patterns from downbursts and microbursts can be either circular or oval, the term straight-line winds is often used because the damage points to a strong wind blowing out of one direction, leveling everything in its path like a steamroller.

SUMMER SOLSTICE

It hits on or near June 21st every year, and it's one of the longest days of the year. When we hit one of these seasonal milestones, do you ever stop and think about why we have seasons? Like so many things in life, it's all a case of perspective, at least when it comes to the Earth and the Sun… and the Earth is always on the move.

We all know that the Earth orbits the Sun. It takes 365.24 days to make it around. We call it a year. But there's a little more to it than that. You see, our spinning little planet is a bit off-kilter. It tilts! In fact, it "leans" at an angle of 23 ½ degrees. In the Northern Hemisphere, where we live, the Earth is tilted toward the Sun during the summer solstice, giving us longer, warmer days. The opposite is true in the Southern Hemisphere, where winter is just settling in.

So how long is the longest day of the year? Darn long in Alaska! In fact, north of the Arctic Circle it's 24 hours long. That's why they call Alaska "the land of the midnight sun." From there, it varies with latitude, getting shorter as you go south. Along the U.S./Canadian border, the Sun can stay out for just over 16 hours and 15 minutes, barring any cloud cover. But if you were to travel down to Florida or Texas, the Sun would only appear for 13 hours and 45 minutes.

OK, here's another question: Is June 21st the hottest day of the year? Well, it could be, if conditions were right, but not as a rule. It continues to warm up through the summer. Strange. If the days are getting shorter again, wouldn't that mean less sun and, therefore, less heat? Not at all. In fact, our warmest time of the year is typically about a month past the solstice.

It's all a case of surpluses and deficits. Sounds like the economy, right? Well, in some ways, the Earth has an energy budget. The Earth accumulates and radiates heat throughout the year. As long as there's more incoming than outgoing heat, we have a surplus and the Earth continues to heat up. This happens during the summer months in either hemisphere. For us, this trend continues until late July. Sure, there's less incoming heat on a daily basis, since the days are growing shorter, but there's still a surplus. And as long as there's a surplus, our weather continues to warm.

From then on, it's like deficit spending. The Northern Hemisphere begins losing more heat than it gains. The deficit grows, we cool off and inexorably move toward fall. That's what the seasons are all about. There's a little something for everyone.

SUN

Ol' Sol (the Sun's real name) is the source of almost all the energy on Earth. It's uneven heating that basically creates the weather. Sounds impressive. But as much as it means to us, the Sun is a very average star. No more than 10% of the stars in the universe are more than 10 times bigger or 10 times smaller than the Sun.

SUN DOGS

This is another optical phenomenon caused by looking at the Sun through the ice crystals in high cirrus-type clouds. Sun dogs, or mock suns, may appear, along with halos, on the ring encircling the Sun, one on each side of the Sun, exactly to its right and left. Sun dogs are usually brightly colored with a reddish tinge on the "sun side" and bluish-white coloration on the outside. When the viewing process results in a complete ring around the Sun, it is called a halo.

H. Michael Mogil

Halo photograph shot at the Outer Banks of North Carolina.

SUNRISE/SUNSET

It's funny how many calls I get about these two. It's as if a minute
here or there makes a great difference to some people. By
definition, in this country at least, sunrise is the moment the very
edge of the sun's disk appears on the eastern horizon. Sunset is,
for all intents and purposes, the instant the disk drops below the
western horizon in the evening. Sunrise and sunset vary
throughout the year, often changing by a minute or two every
couple of days. The summer and winter solstices are the two
longest days of the year in terms of possible minutes of sunshine
from dawn to dusk.

By the way, it may sound strange, but the sky usually becomes
light about a half hour before sunrise and stays light for about a
half hour after sunset.

TEMPERATURE

In the United States, we use a system called the Fahrenheit scale. Water freezes at 32°F and boils at 212°F. Much of the rest of the world uses the Celsius scale… which, of course, makes far more sense. Water freezes at 0°C and boils at 100°C. That's base 10! It doesn't get much easier than that. Except, I don't think in Celsius.

Did you know… that you can use a cricket as a thermometer? It's easy. Count the number of times a cricket chirps in 14 seconds and add 40. This will give you the Fahrenheit temperature at "cricket level" (the ground). Of course, the reading may be two or three degrees higher up where you're standing. The problem might be singling out just one of these noisy denizens of the night. (see **Celsius** and **Fahrenheit**)

THUNDER

Sometimes it sounds like a low flying jet, other times it's more like someone's bowling up there. But thunder is caused by the super-heating of air by a bolt of lightning. The lightning heats the surrounding air to temperatures approaching 50,000°F! This causes the air to expand very rapidly. Since sound travels in waves, the first thing you generally hear is a loud "clap" from the nearest part of the lightning stroke. This is followed by rolls or a deep rumbling from the parts of the lightning stroke that are farther away. Would you believe the beginning and end points of the lightning can be more than five miles apart?

Now, even though it doesn't seem like it, thunder and lightning happen at the same time. But we see the lightning first, then hear the thunder, because light travels much faster than sound. (Think about it. We have planes that have broken the sound barrier, but only the *Starship Enterprise* has broken the speed of light!)

Here's a little game you can play. How can you tell how far away the lightning is? Well, the next time you see a flash of lightning, count the seconds until you first hear the thunder. Divide the number of seconds by five, and you'll know how many miles you are from the lightning. You can also use this little trick to see which way the storm is moving. If the time between the flash and the rumble is less and less, it's coming this way!

At Home

- Stay informed. Be aware of changing weather conditions. (Have a battery operated radio/NOAA Weather radio.)

- Avoid talking on the phone. (Phone lines can conduct electricity.)

- Stay clear of baths and showers. (Metal pipes also conduct electricity.)

- Unplug any sensitive appliances such as TVs, VCRs, and computers. (Lightning strikes may cause power surges.)

Away from Home

- Get out of wide open spaces, don't make yourself a human lightning rod.

- Avoid taking shelter under or near a tree. Trees can easily become lightning rods and their roots extend out for long distances.

- Seek shelter in a car and keep the windows up. Between the car frame and the rubber tires, you will be grounded.

- If there's no shelter at all, find a low spot or squat on the ground in a tucked position.

Thunderstorm Safety Tips

THUNDER SNOW

This one always surprises people... but you can have snow and thunder at the same time. It's especially common around the Great Lakes. Cold, very humid air supplies a key ingredient to the thunderstorm. With a little help from the upper atmosphere, violent churning in these clouds, filled with ice crystals, can create the powerful electric charges that cause lightning and, of course, thunder.

TORNADO

Tornadoes are, at once, nature's most powerful and compelling storms. In short, they represent the most concentrated form of atmospheric energy on the planet. A tornado can pack winds of up to 300 miles per hour... the strongest winds on Earth! Whenever I pay a visit to a local grade school, the subject of tornadoes never fails to come up. One reason is that I always make it a point to talk to kids about tornado safety and what watches and warnings are all about. The funny part is, what these young minds share with me about their own experiences and preconceived notions. The discussion invariably becomes a show and tell of personal and family experiences.

While we all may not have seen a tornado first hand, fortunately I might add, most of us have seen pictures on the evening news, in a book, or have a family member who has had a close brush with this devastating storm. Here in Ohio, who hasn't heard about the infamous Xenia tornado of 1974. On April 3rd and 4th, a dozen tornadoes struck Ohio, killing 37 people while injuring over 2000. Of those, 33 of the dead were from Xenia, as were more than half the injured. Damage from the storm, which lasted a little over half an hour, was close to $3 million a minute! The Xenia storm was part of a "super outbreak" of tornadoes that produced 148 tornadoes.

Ohio is located at the extreme eastern fringe of "tornado alley," a region running from just east of the Rockies to the Gulf Coast. This region of the United States has the dubious distinction of being the most tornado "friendly" area in the world! Tornadoes can occur at any time of the year or any time of day in Ohio. The following pages give you tornado facts and safety tips for Ohio.

Mary Circelli/The Columbus Dispatch

Tornado in Utica, Ohio, May 31,1985.

TORNADO FACTS

Peak tornado season runs from April to June. Historically, these months have produced more than half of Ohio's tornadoes.

Ohio averages 16 tornadoes and five tornado-related deaths each year.

The peak time of day for tornadoes is from 2:00 p.m to 10:00 p.m.

Ninety percent of Ohio's tornadoes come out of the southwestern horizon.

Most tornadoes come from the back portions of strong thunderstorms.

Tornadoes are usually preceded by heavy rains and hail. The larger the hail, the greater the potential for strong storms and possible tornadoes.

The average tornado path in the United States is about five miles long, with a width of 160 to 170 yards. A typical twister affects an area of about one square mile. However, this varies greatly by storm.

Other environmental clues: dark, sometimes greenish sky, a low hanging "wall" cloud, a loud roar, something like a freight train.

Meteorological hedging: None of these rules is foolproof!

By the way: the word "tornado" comes from the Spanish "tornar" meaning to turn and "tronada " meaning thunderstorm.

TORNADO SAFETY TIPS

At Home

- Go to your basement or cellar and take a battery operated radio/TV.

- If you don't have a basement, seek out a small interior room with few windows, preferably a bathroom or a closet. If the bathroom has a tub, climb in and cover yourself with something to protect you from any flying debris.

- In all cases, stay away from windows.

Mobile Homes

- Get out. Leave your mobile home and seek shelter elsewhere. (You really should make this plan well in advance.)

Outside

- First and foremost, try to get inside!

- If there's no shelter nearby, seek out a low spot like a ditch. Lay down as flat as possible and cover your head.

- Do not consider an underpass a good shelter. These can actually help channel the wind.

- A car is NO PROTECTION against a tornado. Never try to outrun a storm. If a tornado is threatening, abandon the vehicle.

At School

- Have a plan, practice, and follow the plan.

TORNADO WARNING

A tornado warning means a tornado or funnel cloud has either been sighted or picked up on radar. This means severe weather is moving through the area and you should be prepared to take immediate shelter.

TORNADO WATCH

A tornado watch is not a guarantee. What this means is that conditions are favorable for tornadoes to develop. It also means be alert to changing weather conditions.

TRIPLE POINT

This is the temperature where water, the key element in so much of our weather, has the odd property of being able to exist as a gas, a solid, and a liquid, all at the same time. The triple point is 32°F or 0°C.

Triple Point

Occluded Front

Cold Front

Warm Front

The triple point is also a position on a storm front where the warm front, cold front, and occluded front meet. (see **Front**)

TROPICAL STORMS

A broad name given to a type of low pressure system that develops in the tropics near the equator. These storms can start as tiny waves and may eventually develop into powerful hurricanes measuring hundreds of miles across. (see **Hurricane**)

TROUGH

The word conjures images of pigs chowing down. But in my world, it refers to an elongated area of low pressure. Troughs act

144

like weak frontal systems in that rising air can lead to rain or showers or, at the very least, a gradual deterioration in weather conditions. On the TV weather map, a trough is shown as a broken, black line that kind of looks like a bunch of dashes.

URBAN HEAT ISLAND

Just like lakes and mountains can affect the weather, so too can big cities. Temperatures in cities tend to be higher than in rural areas or out in the countryside. This is most noticeable on calm, clear nights when it's much warmer downtown than in outlying areas.

Buildings and streets absorb far more of the Sun's heat than trees and open fields. At night, the city actually radiates heat back into the surrounding air. Winds, meanwhile, try to equalize these temperature differences by blowing colder air over cities. As a result, cities can have breezy nights when the wind is barely blowing out in the country.

It also seems that all this warm air rising from the city can have an impact on moving weather systems. How many times have we seen a line of snow showers approaching Columbus from the west. It snows in Bellefontaine, Urbana, Springfield, even London and Marysville. Then, miraculously, nothing happens. We wait, but the forecast just doesn't pan out. Then, as if by magic once again, it snows in Newark, Lancaster, and Zanesville to the east. Only Columbus seems to be left out. The explanation may well be the "urban heat island." And Columbus is an island unto itself.

VAPOR TRAIL

While my favorite use of this term was Bob Uecker describing a long homerun in the movie *Major League*, it's actually a pretty fair description of the cloud-like streamer left behind by jet planes flying in clear, cold, humid air. Also called a contrail, these streamers are created by the water vapor and exhaust gases that planes add to the atmosphere as they fly. If you're ever in Las Vegas, Nevada, where it's sunny most of the time and the airport is very busy, check out the sky. I don't recall a single time where there was not a criss-cross of vapor trails in the sky.

Notice the cloud-like streamers (vapor trails) left behind
by the jet planes flying in clear, cold, humid air

VARIABLE CLOUDS

A shorthand way of saying changeable sky conditions. We use this when the day goes back and forth from sun to clouds and all mixes in between. Alternative descriptions include sun giving way to clouds, intermittent sunshine, and partly-to-mostly sunny.

VERNAL EQUINOX

Spring, by any other name. Sandwiched between winter and summer, spring usually comes as a big relief by the time it rolls around on or about the 20th of March. This is the time when the Sun again crosses the equator and returns to the Northern Hemisphere. (That's our half of the planet.) Welcome back, Mr. Sun! The days are getting longer again and temperatures are starting to warm. Spring is generally thought of as the time when nighttime lows finally climb above freezing and daytime highs start hitting 50°F or more. It's also the time of year when the plants start waking up from their winter slumber.

Popular Myth: You can balance a raw egg on its end on the vernal equinox.

Like all myths, there is some basis in fact here. You **can** balance an egg on its end on the vernal equinox. But there's no astronomical reason that keeps you from doing the same thing any other day of the year!

So where do such urban legends get there start? In most cases, it's almost impossible to track down their roots. But the legend of the balancing egg in this country seems to have been spawned by a magazine article in a popular magazine way back in 1945.

A journalist was on assignment in China when she witnessed a spring ritual involving a crowd of people balancing eggs on Li Chun, the Chinese name for the first day of spring. The United Press picked up the story and *voila*, a legend was born. The funniest part of the story is that the journalist wrote that this occurred on the first day of spring. But spring springs about a month and a half earlier in China than it does in the United States!

For more on this and other astronomical myths and mayhem, check out this web site: http://www.badastronomy.com.

VIRGA

Have you ever noticed those wispy, gray streaks beneath clouds that look like rain but do not appear to be reaching the ground? Well, that's exactly what virga is. It's rain that evaporates into dry air before it reaches the ground. When seen from a distance, the streaks can be mistaken for funnels or tornadoes.

WALL CLOUD

Fortunately, we don't see these very often because they tend to come in tandem with violent spring and summertime thunderstorms... the kind that produce tornadoes. A wall cloud is an abrupt lowering of a cloud from the main cloud base. It takes its name from the fact that it looks like a wall descending from the base of the main cloud. No precipitation is seen underneath, and they tend to develop in severe thunderstorms just prior to tornado formation. Although there's no guarantee that a tornado will hit, a wall cloud is a good sign that this is a powerful and potentially dangerous thunderstorm.

NOAA/National Severe Storms Laboratory

WARM

Talk about subjective! Warm has no definition, per se. It's somewhere between "hot" and "cold." As with many weather definitions, warm is a relative term and is merely a basis for comparison. Thirty-nine degrees Fahrenheit might make for a warm day in the winter, but the same reading would seem frigid in the summer. Warm is the meteorological equivalent of "light" in the dietary sense. (It's only light in comparison to food that's REALLY bad for you.) In other words, there's no legal definition, only a comparative value.

WATERSPOUTS & DUST DEVILS

You might call these distant cousins of the tornado. But even though they resemble tornadoes, waterspouts and dust devils rarely cause death and destruction. Waterspouts are a phenomena, quite common over Lake Erie and the other Great Lakes. They're caused by vertical motion within a cumulus cloud over a large lake. In such cases, a certain amount of spin may develop which, when aided by high relative humidity, can cause a weak funnel to form. If the vortex is strong enough, a spray of water may rise from the lake surface creating a waterspout. Oh sure, they look like tornadoes, but they're more like a weak, baby sister.

© J.H. Golden, 1967

Waterspout near Lower Matecumbe Key, Florida

Dust devils are more of a desert phenomena. They tend to occur on sunny days in late winter over open ground or on very hot days in the summer. If the air near the ground is unstable, it can start to spin as it rises. If the spinning is concentrated enough, the vortex will lift dust, sand, and debris into the air. Oddly enough, there are normally no clouds associated with these mini-tornadoes. This sets them apart from tornadoes and waterspouts. A dust devil may be triggered by little irregularities in the terrain. And, unlike tornadoes, they can spin either clockwise or counterclockwise.

WEATHER

It's my life! We are all affected by it. We're all interested in it. But none of us can do anything about it. Weather covers everything from the Sun to the wind, the winter to the summer, the rain to the snow, and the high to the low. The questions are: Where does the weather come from? What causes it?

The weather is made up of a complex collection of elements. It's caused by the Sun, the tilt of the Earth, the way the Earth revolves around the Sun, the moisture and gases in the air, and the way they heat, mix, and stir. The way all these changing elements work together determines the end result: the weather. Keep in mind, most of these can vary in speed and intensity. The end result is very complex... and difficult to forecast.

WEATHER BALLOONS

When they're not crash landing near Roswell, New Mexico, weather balloons help meteorologists figure out what's going on in the upper levels of the atmosphere, which helps us predict what's going to happen here on the ground. Weather balloons are launched twice a day from hundreds of sites around the world. Loaded with instruments and transmitters, they measure everything from temperature, to moisture, to winds aloft. Many of these balloons rise to nearly 100,000 feet before bursting.

H. Michael Mogil

Trina Heiser of the National Weather Service (NWS) prepares to launch a radiosonde balloon. The balloon (about 5 feet tall at the ground) carries an instrument package to high altitudes. Data is gathered electronically and radioed back to the NWS. Eventually, the balloon expands and bursts; the instrument package returns to Earth gently thanks to an onboard parachute.

WEATHER INSTRUMENTS

How do we measure the weather? There are lots of ways. But to a great extent, it all goes back to the basics of temperature, pressure, relative humidity, and wind. And for basic measurements, you need basic instruments.

Thermometer: Thermometers measure temperature: how hot or cold it is. For our purposes, we usually use a mercury filled thermometer or one filled with red-colored alcohol. Mercury thermometers are the most accurate, and the silver fluid reacts quickly to a change in temperature. The two most common scales used for determining the temperature are Fahrenheit and Celsius.

Barometer: Barometers measure the weight of the air (air pressure). Just like thermometers, many use mercury, though in an inverted tube, to gauge the pressure. At home, aneroid (fluid-less) barometers are far more common. The key with a barometer is not so much the pressure itself, but the trend and speed of the changes. Barometers and altimeters (devices that planes use to tell them how high they are off the ground) are basically the same thing, although they're calibrated differently.

Anemometer/Wind Vane: It takes two, count 'em, two instruments to measure the wind. The anemometer, which looks like a series of spinning cups, tells how fast the wind is blowing. But that's only half the story. You also need a wind vane, like the kind people used to keep on top of their garages, to tell you which way the wind is blowing. If you don't have both, it's like reporting partial sports scores like "Blue Jackets 4." Huh?

Hygrometer: This one gives you the relative humidity. In other words, it tells you whether it's a dry heat or not. The key component of early hygrometers was, of all things, human hair, because of its water absorbing properties. Have you ever heard the expression "I'm having a bad hair day?" Chances are it's humid, and your hair is soaking up water from the atmosphere like a sponge. (This always happens when you have a big date or a job interview!)

WEATHERLINE

469-1010. That's the number to call for an up-to-date, accurate Central Ohio forecast 24 hours a day (614 area code). Automated weatherlines, like automated travel forecasts, movie schedules, and sports hotlines, seem to be the wave of the future. It never ceases to amaze me, but Weatherline receives millions of calls per year!

WIND

No, this isn't what the weatherman's a bag of...

Sure, some of us are, occasionally, filled with hot air. But I'm speaking meteorologically. Wind is the air's way of compensating for pressure differences (see **Barometric Pressure**). You may not be aware, but different parts of the world have their own "pet winds." Some of these winds have the most colorful colloquial names in all of meteorology! From Collada to Kona, Chinook to Sirocco, and from the Haboob to the Simoom, you'd be hard pressed to find better "knik" names for everyday phenomena! A few of my favorites are listed on the next two pages.

Bora: This is a cold wind of the Adriatic, blowing down from high plateaus.

Cat's Paw: This is a weak local breeze that shows itself by rippling the surface of water.

Chinook: "The snow eater!" This is a warm, winter wind that sweeps out of the eastern Rockies toward the central plains of the United States and Canada causing snow to melt incredibly fast!

Collada: This is a strong northerly wind that blows over the Gulf of California. (Not to be confused with a Piña Colada!)

Doctor: This is a term referring to a cool, invigorating (feel good) sea breeze in tropical climates.

Doldrums: While this may well be a state of mind, we occasionally fall into, it's also the area of very light winds around the equator (between the trade wind belts).

Foehn: A warm, dry wind characteristic of mountain regions. The air warms as it rushes down a mountain slope and into a valley. (If you live in the valley, you might call it a wind that "foehns" home.)

Haboob: This is the Sudanese word for a type of desert wind blowing sand and dust.

Knik: This is a strong southeast wind near Palmer, Alaska. I guess you could say that Palmer has a knack for kniks. (Not to be confused with a *New York Knick*.)

Winds

Kona: Sure, it's a popular kind of Hawaiian coffee, but it's also an especially oppressive and sultry, southwestern Hawaiian wind!

Mistral: This is a stormy, cold northern wind blowing down from the mountains along the Mediterranean or Adriatic coasts. (If a mistral wind whistles through the trees, would you call it a minstral wind?)

Norther: This is a strong, cold Canadian wind that descends southward over the United States, sometimes to the Gulf of Mexico or Mexico's east coast.

Santa Ana: These are mountain pass winds from California. They start as north or east winds in the deserts and plateaus of southern California. They warm as they cross the southern ranges and move toward the coast.

Shamal: This is a northwesterly wind from the Persian Gulf.

Simoom: This is a nasty one. It's an intensely hot and dry wind in Asian and African deserts.

Sirocco: This one's kind of generic. It's a warm wind in the Mediterranean that typically blows from a warm region toward low pressure in a colder region (also a kind of Volkswagen).

Beaufort Wind Speed Scale

Developed in 1805 by Sir Francis Beaufort of England

force	knot	mph	kph	sea term	sea conditions	on-land appearances
0	<=1	<=1	<=2	calm	mirror-like water surface	smoke rises vertically
1	1–3	1–3	2–6	light air or wind	small ripples on surface	smoke drifts and leaves rustle
2	4–6	4–7	7–11	light breeze	small glassy wavelets	wind felt on face
3	7–10	8–11	12–19	gentle breeze	large wavelets, some white caps	flags extended, leaves move
4	11–16	12–18	20–30	moderate breeze	small waves, frequent white caps	dust and small branches move
5	17–21	19–24	31–39	fresh breeze	moderate waves, many white caps, some spray possible	small trees begin to sway
6	22–27	25–31	40–50	strong breeze	large waves, white caps all around, some spray	large branches move, wires whistle
7	28–33	32–38	51–61	near gale	seas heap up the waves, some foam streaks off waves tops	trees in motion, resistance felt when walking
8	34–40	39–46	62–74	gale	moderately high waves, edges of crests break off in spindrift, foam makes well defined streaks	walking impeded
9	41–47	47–54	75–87	strong gale	high waves, dense streaks of spray, visibility affected	structural damage may occur
10	48–55	55–63	88–101	full gale or storm	very high waves, surface white with spray and foam, visibility reduced	trees uprooted, structural damage likely
11	56–63	64–73	102–117	violent storm	exceptionally high waves, small to medium ships obscured, visibility limited	damage to structures wide spread
12	64–71	74–82	118–132	hurricane (start of)	air filled with foam and spray, sea white, visibility restricted	severe structural damage to buildings, wide spread devastation, flooding

WIND CHILL

Wind chill has to do with a loss of body heat due to the combined effects of wind and cold. Can wind chill freeze your pipes? No. Does wind chill affect your car starting? No. Can wind chill kill you? Absolutely. As the wind increases, heat is carried away from the body at a much greater rate. As a result, body temperature drops. This can lead to hypothermia. In a nutshell, wind chill is the effect of wind and temperature on the rate of heat loss for a human body, which depends upon the amount of exposed skin.

A wind chill advisory is issued when wind-chill temperatures are expected to be 30 degrees below zero (-30°F) or colder. For example, if the afternoon high is expected to reach 20°F, but there's going to be a 25 mile per hour (mph) wind, the wind chill factor would be 15 degrees below zero (-15°F)! At least, that's what it would feel like to any exposed skin. Now, let's take the same scenario, but drop the temperature another 10 degrees. The wind chill would drop to -29°F, putting you into the danger category. That means exposed skin is in imminent danger of freezing. Once the Sun sets, let's say we are expecting another 10 degree drop, to where the thermometer reads zero. If that same 25 mph wind keeps blowing, the wind chill drops to -44°F!

Keep in mind, the wind chill index (WCI) is computed based on sustained winds. What if the wind is gusty? Well, that won't show up in our wind chill reports, but trust me, you'll feel it. Take that last case. If the temperature is zero with a 25 mph wind, the wind chill index is -44°F. But what if there were 40 mph gusts along with it? Now the wind chill drops to -53°F! Any way you slice it, that's COLD! If you have to go out in weather like this, be sure to dress properly. Wear layered clothing, hats, gloves, and scarves. This will help prevent hypothermia. Even with precautions, it's always best to limit your exposure to such intense cold.

Wind Chill

Wind Chill Temperature (°F)	Terminology
> 15 – ≤ 32	cold
> 0 – ≤ 15	very cold
> -20 – ≤ 0	bitter cold
≤ -20	extreme cold

	Actual Air Temperature (°F)								
	20	15	10	5	0	-5	-10	-15	-20
Apparent Temperature									
Wind Speed (mph) 5	16	12	7	0	-5	-10	-15	-21	-26
10	3	-3	-9	-15	-22	-27	-34	-40	-46
15	-5	-11	-18	-25	-31	-38	-45	-51	-58
20	-10	-17	-24	-31	-39	-46	-53	-60	-67
25	-15	-22	-29	-36	-44	-51	-59	-66	-74
30	-18	-25	-33	-41	-49	-56	-64	-71	-79
35	-20	-27	-35	-43	-52	-58	-67	-74	-82
40	-21	-29	-37	-45	-53	-60	-69	-76	-84
45	-22	-30	-38	-46	-54	-62	-70	-78	-85

source: National Weather Service

WIND SHEAR

This is the one we always seem to hear about during news stories about plane crashes. And frankly, wind shear can be a very dangerous thing, especially when flying. The dangerous thing about it is that you can't see it. Wind shear is a sharp change in wind speed over distance, which can occur vertically or horizontally. If the change in velocity is sharp enough, it can actually cause a twisting motion in the air, making it even more dangerous and unpredictable.

Whereas horizontal wind shear means a change in wind velocity over distance, vertical wind shear means there's a change in velocity with height. Vertical wind shear can play havoc with airplanes, especially if it occurs close to the ground. A strong downward shear can be enough to cause a plane crash. Detection of areas of wind shear by ground based Doppler radar can also help pinpoint areas of air turbulence, another concern of pilots.

WINTER

It's inevitable. Anyone who has lived in the great state of Ohio knows all about winter. From the snow belt of extreme northeastern Ohio, to the more moderate regions of central and southern Ohio, to the artificial dividing line between flurries and heavy snow called I-70, we all know a little something about winter weather.

The Great Blizzard of 1978 remains one of the worst examples of winter weather. More than 50 Ohioans died, and parts of the state were paralyzed for days. While such storms are rare, the potential is always there. As a result, I think it's important to be familiar with the terms we use to keep you informed as to any potential threat.

Folklore: "When squirrels early start to hoard, winter will pierce us like a sword."

160

WINTER DRIVING

Winter and driving. The two really don't go together. Unfortunately, there's no way to avoid it. But, when road conditions are bad, or expected to deteriorate, it's best to remember a few basic safe driving tips.

Don't OVER-do it. Don't over accelerate, over-break, or over-steer.

Bridges get icy and slick before roads do.

Leave ample stopping distance between you and the car in front of you!

Keep your windows clear, inside and out.

Turn your lights on in snow. A good rule: If you need your wipers, your lights should be on. (Be sure to clean off your headlights and tail lights before driving.)

Keep your gas tank at least half full. This will help prevent fuel line freeze-up and could be a life-saver if you get stranded.

Don't pump ABS (anti-lock brake system) brakes. Just apply firm pressure to stop.

Never decrease tire pressure to try to get better traction. This will just wear out your tires.

Avoid parallel parking when icy. It's easy to get stuck while turning your wheels.

Winter Driving Tips

If you do get into trouble in a snow storm, the best thing to do is stay with your car. The car will provide shelter, but here are a couple of survival tips. (Just in case.)

Snow Storm Survival

Tie a red cloth to your antenna, driver door handle or outside mirror. This will help signal anyone who might pass by. Lighting a flare works too.

Keep the exhaust pipe clear of snow. Carbon monoxide poisoning may result if the tailpipe is clogged.

Run the engine and heater no more than ten minutes every hour. (Leave a window cracked for ventilation.)

Keep a blanket handy for extra warmth. If you're caught without one, seat covers or floor mats can help keep you warm. (see Winter Emergency Car Kit)

Don't eat snow. This will only make you colder. Melt it down in a cup or can to be used as drinking water later.

WINTER EMERGENCY CAR KIT

Keep an emergency kit in your trunk, just in case. Here are some items you should think about including:

- 2 blankets (at least)
- waterproof matches and candles
- extra clothing, especially boots and mittens
- a steel shovel, sand, and rope for a lifeline
- dry food rations like raisins, nuts, and candy
- a flashlight with spare batteries and emergency flares
- garbage bags to be used as insulation against the wind
- a metal coffee can for storing small items and for melting snow for drinking
- change for pay phones

WINTER SOLSTICE

Welcome to the shortest day of the year. The winter solstice hits on or about December 21st. In the Northern Hemisphere, where we live, the Earth is now tilted away from the Sun. Bottom line: the days grow shorter and colder. At the solstice, the Sun is only about 25 degrees above the southern horizon at noon in Ohio. We're getting far less daylight and at such a low angle, the Sun's energy is spread out over a much larger area. Therefore, a chill sets in. Time to check the fire wood! By the way, do you know where your heavy coat is?

WINTER STORM WARNING

A warning means "here it comes." They're issued to warn folks that bad winter weather now appears imminent. These are usually issued 6–12 hours in advance of the approaching storm and generally follow a winter storm watch unless a storm has developed unusually quickly. A winter storm warning means heavy snow, freezing rain, or heavy sleet is expected. These do not make for safe travel conditions.

WINTER STORM WATCH

As with severe thunderstorm watches, a winter storm watch means conditions are right for severe winter weather to develop, such as heavy snow, freezing rain, or heavy sleet. A watch is usually issued 12–36 hours in advance of the approaching system. Again, because there is some distance involved which could affect the way the storm tracks, a winter storm watch is not a guarantee of severe winter weather.

WINTER WEATHER ADVISORY

Sounds pretty generic. Right? Still, this is one of those things you hear about all the time during the winter season. This type of advisory is issued when two or more of the following conditions are expected to occur at the same time: dense fog, dangerous wind chill, freezing rain, snow, or blowing and drifting snow. The National Weather Service tends to issue this type of advisory when temperatures during a storm hover around the freezing mark, making a mix of these conditions more likely.

WOOLYBEAR CATERPILLAR

Like that darned groundhog, here's another garden pest that returns to haunt the meteorologist year-in and year-out. But you gotta love 'em, right? The woolybears are supposed to be the harbingers of winter. A fat woolybear means expect a cold winter. By contrast, a skinny little caterpillar foreshadows a mild winter. Then, of course, there's the band on its back. A thick band supposedly indicates below normal snowfall. A narrow band (say a half inch or less), however, means to expect lots of snow. Or so they say...

WORLD WIDE WEB (WWW)

Anyone who is ANYONE seems to have a web site these days. 10TV is no exception! And, as you might expect, you can get your daily dose of weather right here, any time you want. Our address on the world wide web is: **http://www.10TV.com**

Any way you look at it, there's plenty of weather on the web...

One of the most useful web sites I know, if you're looking for climate or forecast information is the National Weather Service's Wilmington Web Site: **http://www.nws.noaa.gov/er/iln/iln.htm**

For folks looking for information further north in Ohio, NWS Cleveland also has a web page: **http://www.csuohio.edu/nws**

Taking that one step further, you can get to any NWS web site by visiting: **http://srh.noaa.gov/tlh/wwwnws.html**

Even the National Oceanic and Atmospheric Administration (NOAA) has a web site: **http://www.noaa.gov**

Visit the Storm Prediction Center at: **http://www.spc.noaa.gov**

Here you'll find information on severe weather watches and warnings across the country.

If tropical weather interests you, check out the National Hurricane Center's Tropical Prediction Center at: **http://nhc.noaa.gov**

If you have an interest in tornadoes, you might want to check out Tornado Project online at: **http://www.tornadoproject.com**

If it's meteorology you're after, check out The Ohio State University's Meteorology Club web page at: **http://twister.sbs.ohio-state.edu**

Check out this site: **http://www.weatherpoint.com/sentinel**

The Orlando Sentinel hosts this weather page for those interested in Disney World or tropical weather.

As I said, there are many such sites on the information super highway. Have fun surfing the net! By the way, web addressed do have the vexing habit of changing from time to time. So don't be surprised if you've book-marked any of the above, only to one day find that the site has up and moved on you.

X

XENIA

Xenia is a lovely town, located in the heart of Ohio's Greene County. Unfortunately, it's probably best known around the state for some of the most devastating tornadoes to ever hit Ohio.

The day was April 3, 1974. An F5 Tornado ripped through downtown Xenia, killing 33 people and causing 75 million dollars in damage.

Xenia was certainly not alone that day. This was just one of dozens of tornadoes that hit all across the country in what has been dubbed the "super outbreak." To this day, it remains the single worst single-day outbreak in United States history.

Then, in the year 2000, mother nature struck again. This time, an F4 tornado left an eight- to nine-mile path of destruction through Greene County, passing through the northwest corner of the city. One man died as a result of the storm, and once again, many homes and businesses were totally demolished.

Damage caused by the Xenia Tornado, April 4, 1974.

X-RAY

It always scares me in the doctor's office when I need one of these and the technician makes me wear a lead smock and then quickly leaves the room. But X-rays are a natural part of our environment. This is the part of the electromagnetic spectrum that has a very short wavelength (shorter than visible light). X-rays can penetrate solid objects and, when absorbed by a gas, ionize it.

YEAR

The amount of time it takes the Earth to revolve around the Sun. To be precise, it's 365 days, six hours, nine minutes, and 9.5 seconds. Because the actual year exceeds our calendar year of 365 days, we add a day every four years, making that year a leap year.

ZONAL FLOW

I throw this in every once and awhile when talking about our fast-changing weather. Here in the Northern Hemisphere, air generally flows west to east. That's why most of our storms come from the west. Well, a zonal flow describes west-to-east air movement along a latitudinal component of the existing flow. The result tends to be extremely inconsistent weather, where no two days seem to be alike.

ZULU

No, this is not the navigator on the original *Star Trek*. That was SULU. Zulu is the term referring to "universal time" or Greenwich mean time (GMT). Weather maps around the world are all based on Zulu or Universal Time Coordinate (UTC), so that no matter where you live, you know exactly what time the observations were taken or the precise time of the forecast. The only catch is that we must all convert ZULU time back into our local time. Here in Ohio, we're either four or five hours earlier than Zulu time, depending on daylight savings time. Use of Zulu time is widespread in the scientific and military communities.

INDEX